BERRIES

Edible

Series Editor: Andrew F. Smith

EDIBLE is a revolutionary series of books dedicated to food and drink that explores the rich history of cuisine. Each book reveals the global history and culture of one type of food or beverage.

Already published

Apple Erika Janik · *Banana* Lorna Piatti-Farnell
Barbecue Jonathan Deutsch and Megan J. Elias · *Beef* Lorna Piatti-Farnell
Beer Gavin D. Smith · *Berries* Heather Arndt Anderson
Brandy Becky Sue Epstein · *Bread* William Rubel · *Cake* Nicola Humble
Caviar Nichola Fletcher · *Champagne* Becky Sue Epstein
Cheese Andrew Dalby · *Chillies* Heather Arndt Anderson
Chocolate Sarah Moss and Alexander Badenoch
Cocktails Joseph M. Carlin · *Corn* Michael Owen Jones
Curry Colleen Taylor Sen · *Dates* Nawal Nasrallah
Doughnut Heather Delancey Hunwick · *Dumplings* Barbara Gallani
Edible Flowers Constance L. Kirker and Mary Newman
Eggs Diane Toops · *Fats* Michelle Phillipov
Figs David C. Sutton · *Game* Paula Young Lee
Gin Lesley Jacobs Solmonson · *Hamburger* Andrew F. Smith
Herbs Gary Allen · *Herring* Kathy Hunt · *Honey* Lucy M. Long
Hot Dog Bruce Kraig · *Ice Cream* Laura B. Weiss · *Lamb* Brian Yarvin
Lemon Toby Sonneman · *Lobster* Elisabeth Townsend
Melon Sylvia Lovegren · *Milk* Hannah Velten · *Moonshine* Kevin R. Kosar
Mushroom Cynthia D. Bertelsen · *Nuts* Ken Albala · *Offal* Nina Edwards
Olive Fabrizia Lanza · *Onions and Garlic* Martha Jay
Oranges Clarissa Hyman · *Oyster* Carolyn Tillie · *Pancake* Ken Albala
Pasta and Noodles Kantha Shelke · *Pickles* Jan Davison · *Pie* Janet Clarkson
Pineapple Kaori O'Connor · *Pizza* Carol Helstosky
Pomegranate Damien Stone · *Pork* Katharine M. Rogers
Potato Andrew F. Smith · *Pudding* Jeri Quinzio · *Rice* Renee Marton
Rum Richard Foss · *Salad* Judith Weinraub · *Salmon* Nicolaas Mink
Sandwich Bee Wilson · *Sauces* Maryann Tebben · *Sausage* Gary Allen
Seaweed Kaori O'Connor · *Shrimp* Yvette Florio Lane
Soup Janet Clarkson · *Spices* Fred Czarra · *Sugar* Andrew F. Smith
Sweets and Candy Laura Mason · *Tea* Helen Saberi · *Tequila* Ian Williams
Truffle Zachary Nowak · *Vodka* Patricia Herlihy · *Water* Ian Miller
Whiskey Kevin R. Kosar · *Wine* Marc Millon

Berries

A Global History

Heather Arndt Anderson

REAKTION BOOKS

This book is dedicated to my mother Debbie, who, like me,
enjoyed eating feral berries as a young Cascadian wildling.

Published by Reaktion Books Ltd
Unit 32, Waterside
44–48 Wharf Road
London N1 7UX, UK
www.reaktionbooks.co.uk

First published 2018
Copyright © Heather Arndt Anderson 2018

Printed and bound in China

A catalogue record for this book is available from the British Library

ISBN 978 1 78023 895 1

Contents

Introduction 7

1 Botany 9

2 Berry-lore 26

3 Picking and Growing 47

4 Dishes and Drinks 72

5 Poison and Panacea 116

Appendix: Botanical Descriptions 131

Recipes 139

References 151

Bibliography 157

Websites and Associations 159

Acknowledgements 163

Photo Acknowledgements 165

Index 169

Introduction

There are few more welcome sights to a hungry hiker than a bush heavy with ripe berries. Humans aren't the only creatures to know the joys of berries; they're loved by birds, squirrels and insects; they sufficiently fatten bears for hibernation through the winter. North America commercially produces far more berries than any other region in the world – more than two million tonnes in 2012 – with Russia coming in a distant second place at 710,000 tonnes. As their national symbol the bear does, Russians, too, adore berries; their word for 'buttocks', *yagoditsy*, literally translates as 'little berries'.

Because berry-producing plants tend to prefer moist, acidic humus (especially in volcanic soils), they grow best in the temperate regions of the world which also support vast forests. Berries may not be fussy about where they grow, but they are so delicate that they are largely produced for local consumption rather than global shipping. No berries rank in the top ten fruits produced worldwide, but their following is ardent. Berries are much more than mere pie fillings and jams: they're sacred medicine, spiritual totems and deadly weapons.

So many of us hailing from northern climes have fond childhood memories involving berries: filling empty margarine

...s with wild blackberries from grassy urban alleys and weedy field edges; eating dewy, coral-hued berries from a (poisonous) yew and somehow avoiding death; cruelly tricking a younger brother into eating bittersweet nightshade berries just to watch his face screw up in disgust; trying mealy hawthorn berries more than once to see if they were worth the spines, and deciding that they were perhaps not. Some pick them on pastoral farmlands, some in the hallowed forests, some on scabby marshes. We have done this since time immemorial, and will for ever more.

This little book cannot possibly provide a comprehensive discussion of each and every berry, but it will attempt to shed light on some of the better-loved berries of the world and some of the compelling reasons they have been so adored. Be they a staple foodstuff, a fad or exalted in ancient, sacred lore, berries are part of our human history.

I
Botany

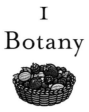

A berry is rightfully defined as any fruit whose seeds are enclosed in fleshy pulp and covered with a thin skin. But a berry can be so much more. Everyone knows what one means when one speaks of berries. Most people will not think of a banana or an orange when a berry is mentioned, and nor will most fret that a strawberry is, botanically speaking, something else entirely.

Berries are a counter-intuitive and perplexing lot. Botanically, 'berry' is a broadly defined term that includes tomatoes, persimmons, coffee beans and kiwifruit. Mind-bogglingly, it also includes the sturdy, rind-bearing fruit known as pepos, such as cucumbers, melons and papaya. A banana is technically a leathery berry, and segmented fruits with a pliable rind, such as citrus, are a type of berry called a hesperidium. The odd-looking cherimoya (custard apple) is an aggregate of berries. Berries are indehiscent; that is, they do not split open when ripe, as do milkweed pods, say. Botanically, a berry-like fruit is said to be baccate, meaning 'pearl-like'. This is unrelated to the word 'bacchanal', an occasion of wild and wine-drunken revelry, named for the Graeco-Roman wine god Bacchus. (Grapes are also true berries, but they warrant their own book and are therefore ignored here.)

Berries for sale at a farmer's market in California.

Technically, the juniper berry is nothing more than a soft cone. Strictly speaking, the term 'berry' does not apply to the blackberry (an aggregate of tiny individual fruits called drupelets) or the mulberry (a multiple fruit). Nor does it describe the strawberry (an aggregate accessory fruit; the fleshy part grows from the flower's receptacle, not the ovaries). The fruits of these may technically be something else, but it would be pedantic to argue that they aren't berries. In this culinary sense (and common convention), they certainly are.

The word 'berry' is, happily, correctly used to define some fruits that people already consider berries. Huckleberries, cranberries, lingonberries, blueberries, bilberries and so on (all *Vaccinium* spp.) are all true berries, as are gooseberries and their currant cousins (*Ribes* spp.). Elderberries are real berries, as are tart barberries and goji berries. For the intents and purposes of this book, berries are the sweet, juicy, round little fruits that make humble yoghurt and porridges more delicious, and gild the lily of a cake. Here are the world's favourites, sorted taxonomically.

Rose-family Berries

The Rosaceae, or rose family, is a large, cosmopolitan plant family that includes many beloved berries: strawberries, brambles, serviceberries, rowans and hawthorns. Based on their fruit's anatomy, strawberries and caneberries fall into their own subfamily, while chokeberries, rowan berries and serviceberries are in another.

For aeons, strawberries have grown wild throughout the world's temperate regions (and a few tropical places), comprising more than twenty species of juicy, mostly red fruits. Although they are not botanically a berry, one would be hard pressed to find any fruit more emblematic of one. Wild berries tend to be quite tiny and flavourful, while sugar content and

Fresh Oregon strawberries.

flavour intensity tends to be somewhat diminished with increased size. Japanese growers have developed pink- and white-skinned varieties, as well as some of the biggest – the largest strawberry on record came from a Japanese farm.

The name 'strawberry' has long been something of a mystery. 'How well this name indicates the now prevailing practice of English gardeners laying straw under the berry in order to bring it to perfection, and prevent it from touching the earth,' wrote one botanist,

> which without that precaution it naturally does . . . making us almost forget that in this instance 'straw' has nothing to do with the practice alluded to, but is an obsolete past-participle of 'to strew', in allusion to the [growing] habit of the plant.[1]

Whereas strawberries are represented by only about twenty species, the blackberry clan (*Rubus* spp.) includes hundreds. In 1885 Swedish botanist Fredrik Wilhelm Christian Areschoug wrote that there existed, in Western Europe alone, a 'well-nigh inexhaustible abundance of forms of this genus'.[2] Decades later, another authoritative text on the subject, *Rubi of Great Britain and Ireland* (1958), lists 391 species in the British Isles alone. Brambles are an exponentially populous group. There are so many brambles that the act of studying them has its own name: batology.

Brambles, or cane berries, include many hundreds of wild and cultivated shrubs and vines that are wont to poke and snag the unwary forager. The genus is comprised of raspberries, blackberries, salmonberries, thimbleberries, dewberries, cloudberries, wineberries, stone brambles and more. It includes innumerable American and British hybrids and varieties such as loganberry, youngberry, olallieberry,

Eighteenth-century illustration of a raspberry bush.

Raspberry Bush   1. Flower   Rubus idaeus
Eliz. Blackwell delin. sculp. et Pinx   2. Fruit

boysenberry, tayberry, marionberry, tummelberry, veitchberry, silvanberry and hildaberry.

Most bramble plants grow on vines covered in spines. Raspberries were called hindberries in the olden days, referring to their gentle, doe-like hornlessness; by contrast, thorny blackberries were known as hartberries, after the stag's antlers. Pity the poor fool who catches a spiny tripwire across the ankles while walking through the woods in trainers instead of boots.

Serviceberries, also known as saskatoon berries, shadberries or juneberries, are another member of the rose family.

e plants are widely variable, but the spherical fruits typically
all resemble miniature reddish to dark-bluish-purple apples.

Although the Latin name *Amelanchier* comes from the old
French word for medlar (another edible rose cousin), the city
of Saskatoon, Saskatchewan, is named after the saskatoon
berry – an Anglicized version of the Cree word *misâskwatômina*,
meaning 'fruit of the tree of many branches'. One interesting (if dubious) etymology states that the name serviceberry
derives from its being a harbinger of spring, blooming when
the ground has thawed enough to dig graves and hold burial
services for those who have died during the winter. Another
traditional etymology says the name shadberry comes from
the fact that the plant blooms when the shad begin to run in
the rivers to their spawning grounds.

Rowan (*Sorbus* spp.), also known as mountain ash, chequer
tree or service tree (not to be confused with *Amelanchier*), is
a small tree that grows throughout the temperate regions of
the Northern Hemisphere. The common name mountain

Rowan berries.

ash comes from the tree's preference for moderate to high elevations, and from the fact that its feather-like leaves somewhat resemble those of an ash tree (*Fraxinus* spp.). Its other name, chequer, comes from the Old French *eschequier*, meaning a chessboard or chequered counting table (as in the British Exchequer); this has been said to come from the chequered pattern of the bark on mature rowan trees.

The fruits, according to Pliny the Elder, 'groweth thicke among the branches' in clusters of pomes that range from sunshine-yellow to vermilion.[3] There are two basic types of rowan: those that are delicious eaten raw (such as the ones mentioned by Pliny) and those that are best left to jams and jellies. Rosy rowanberry jelly is a delectable addition to any table bearing a venison or lamb roast, or a loaf of good brown bread and Wensleydale cheese.

Like persimmons or quinces, rowans are usually too astringent to eat until they have bletted (been softened by frost). However, once the low temperatures bring out the sugars, rowans have the sweetness and meatiness of dates. The crab-apple-like fruits of the species called service tree are particularly relished as a fruit to be eaten straight from the hand; they are known in Germany as *Speierling*, typically sold fully bletted and a welcome addition to the sweet *Apfelwein* (apple wine) of Hesse.

Similar in growth to the rowan is the hawthorn. Also known as thornapple or haw berry, the hawthorn is a red, starchy berry borne on stems well studded with the stout thorns that give the plant half its name; the other half of the name comes from the Old English word *haw*, meaning 'hedge'.

Another of hawthorn's names, May tree, comes with its own slogan – 'Ne'er cast a cloot 'til May's oot'– a helpful reminder to keep one's clothes on until warmer weather brings hawthorn's blooms. Hawthorn is also known as 'bread and

Hawthorn berries.

butter berry' in the UK, but seeing as they taste rather mealy and bland, it must be the fruit's starchiness that garners this nickname.

In *Nature Near London* (1883), the English nature writer Richard Jefferies described the haw fruits during one recent prolific 'berry year' as having been 'exceptionally large'–weighing apple-like on their branches. He lamented, however, that they weren't nearly as edible as apples, and that even the birds seemed only to eat them as a last resort, when food is scarce in the winter. Nonetheless, Jefferies wrote, 'the hawthorn is a part of natural English life – country life. It stands side by side with the Englishman.'[4]

Blueberry and its Kin (*Vaccinium* spp. &c.)

The Vaccinia are the hundred or so species of blueberries, huckleberries, cranberries, lingonberries, whortleberries, bilberries and salal that grow throughout the temperate and boreal regions of the world. They all like acidic soils and produce blackish or bluish (occasionally reddish) berries that are esculent and wholesome.

Besides tasting nice when cooked, the berries are naturally high in pectin, making them an obvious fit for jams and jellies. The high pectin is responsible for cranberry sauce's tendency to maintain its perfectly ridged cylindrical shape when extruded from its tin. The berries of bog blueberry, according to nineteenth-century botanist John Claudius Loudon, can cause headaches and giddiness. Although it is likely a fungus on the skin that causes the ailment, it was evidently occasionally employed in nineteenth-century England, Siberia and Sweden specifically to that end, as a buzz-inducing additive to beer and spirits.

Several other of its kin are relished throughout the cooler climes of Europe and the Americas. Crowberry (called 'blackberry' in Labrador, Canada; *Empetrum nigrum*) resembles a heather with spherical black berries congregating at the ends of the stems. It's also in Labrador where the stems and branches of crowberry are burned to smoke salmon. *Gaylussacia* spp. are what folks in the eastern and southern portions of the United States call huckleberries, and their flavour and uses are the same. These grow wild as far south as the Andes and the mountains of Brazil.

The evergreen salal (*Gaultheria shallon*) was similarly used by the people of the Pacific Northwest, with its leaves employed in cooking and the berries mashed with dried salmon and venison suet into pemmican cakes. Wintergreen or teaberry (*G. procumbens* and other species) is another member of the genus used by Native Americans; though its ethnobotanical use was predominantly medicinal, the mildly sweet berries have long been a welcome sight to foragers. Nineteenth-century horticulturist James Vick sang its praises:

Ah, the Wintergreen, with its berries and crispy, green leaves, so spicily tempting to school boy and girl epicures. Any child who has ever stood ankle deep in a bed of Wintergreen, will always remember just how the brown woods looked in those days when he filled his pockets and dinnerpail with leaves to chew and berries to eat.[5]

Gooseberries and Currants (*Ribes* spp.)

Ribes spp. include the Worcesterberry, which originate on the Pacific Northwest coast, and the jostaberry, a German hybrid between currants (*Johannisbeere*) and gooseberries (*Stachelbeere*). The name *Ribes* comes from the Persian or Arabic word *ribas*, meaning 'acid-tasting' – an apt description of the berry's tart flavour.

Currants and gooseberries grow wild all over Europe and North America, throughout Asia and in northwestern Africa. Currants are typically red or black (sometimes white), and

Wild Norwegian bilberry.

Black elderberries on the bush.

gooseberries translucent green, with sparse, fine hairs and pretty longitudinal stripes. Like cranberries and lingonberries, currants are tart and high in pectin, making an excellent jelly to accompany strong-flavoured meats and game. Bright-flavoured gooseberries can be pickled and served with oily fish, as the Scandinavians do, or with curd rice, as in India.

Most currants are either dried or turned into jam and jellies, but they are widely cultivated and consumed. Gooseberries, however, enjoy more of a cult following. They are historically beloved in England, and were turned into sparkling wine by the descendants of Vikings, but, as cookbook author Jessup Whitehead wrote in 1889, 'it is a fruit of but little consequence in the United States.'[6]

Elderberry (*Sambucus* spp.)

Arborescent elderberry shrubs grow in forest understoreys and on field edges, tempting cedar waxwings and other feathered sots with their over-ripening fruit. (It is perhaps owing to elderberries' habit of readily fermenting on the bush that they are so widely used in winemaking.) Because they have just one little pip each, elder's tiny fruits are botanically drupes, not berries. They can be purplish-black, blue or red (the last are poisonous), and they are rather seedy and insipid unless cooked or turned to wine. Before using them, their tiny stems must be removed, a tedious task. Nonetheless, wild elderberries have been adored throughout the Northern Hemisphere for millennia. While they haven't historically been as loved in America as in Europe, in the late nineteenth century the u.s. Department of Agriculture sang their praises: 'Let the elderberry be considered as entitled to a place on our list of small fruits, if we do here place it almost at the bottom of our list.'[7]

Mulberry (*Morus* spp.)

Mulberries were once widespread throughout northern Africa, the Middle East, southern Europe and the Mediterranean, plus South Asia. They were introduced to Britain and the burgeoning American colonies in the mid-seventeenth century to feed silk moths, but silk culture never really took off in the colonies as hoped, and the enterprise was soon abandoned for the production of cotton. None of this was the mulberry's fault, however. Silkworms are just fussy.

Fortunately, the new population of introduced black mulberry trees produced delicious fruit that somewhat resembles a blackberry and makes superb sorbet and preserves. Many of the other species produce fruit that is also quite edible, be it red, dark purple or white (though these ones are less flavourful).

Oddballs and Misfits

Closely related to tomatoes, potatoes and the not-so-friendly nightshades beloved by witches and poisoners (belladonna and deadly nightshade), black nightshade berries (*Solanum nigrum*, *S. retroflexum* and *S. scabrum*) have been eaten around the world for millennia, particularly in Africa, Europe and the Mediterranean, but also in China and the Indian subcontinent. Volga Germans settling in the American Breadbasket brought seeds with them from Russia between the 1890s and 1920s; though they are not commonly grown these days, they do grow weedily, and their fruit makes excellent pie and filling for ravioli-like *maultaschen*.

Also called wonderberry, sunberry, stubbleberry, *chichique-lite* and *gsoba*, they are not to be confused with whortleberries, which, like black nightshade berries, are also purportedly called *Schwartzbeeren* (this confusion may be related to another of their nicknames being 'garden huckleberry'). The berries (true berries!) are perfect spheres, starting out green and toxic and ripening to an edible, dark purplish-black. 'I'll not say they are the *best* that was,' wrote one gardener to *Gleanings in Bee Culture Magazine* in 1909, 'but I will say that I never ate any thing in pies or sauce that tasted any better.'[8]

Another member of the nightshade family, goji berries (aka wolfberries), have received recent attention as pillars of nutritional healing, but the plant has been cultivated in China since at least the Shang Dynasty approximately four thousand years ago.[9] It grows wild in British hedgerows, thanks to the Duke of Argyll having introduced it in the 1730s (it's still sometimes called 'Duke of Argyll's tea plant'). The vermilion berry looks like a tiny chilli. It's typically dried, giving it the appearance of a red raisin, and the tart fruits are used to fortify rice porridge and tonic soups.

A relative of the edible Oregon grape of the Pacific Northwest, 'the barberry is so well-armed with spines that one would scarcely expect animals to feed on it,' wrote one botanist in 1921.[10] Truly, the barberry is a nasty little shrub. Not only are its small leaves fully rimmed with spines, but each leaf node also bears three or more, each nearly a centimetre in length. Thanks to an ample supply of tart malic acid, even the berries, elongated and carmine-red, are sharp.

Nonetheless, the people of Rouen, France, have a cherished confiture made from a seedless variety of the tart fruits, which they call *marmalade d'épine-vinette*, and Israeli cookbook author Yotam Ottolenghi considers the barberry one of his favourite ingredients. Close relatives, known interchangeably as *calafate* or *michay*, are used in Patagonia for jam as well. Iranians prefer another species, *B. integerrima*, which they dry into a raisin called *zereshk* and cook with chicken and rice dishes.

Blue honeysuckle berries, also known as haskap or honeyberries.

Japanese barberries in the snow.

English cookbooks from the sixteenth century employ the berry to a similar end, as seen in a chicken pie in *A Proper Newe Booke of Cokerye* (1575). Early American cookbooks, including the first one, Amelia Simmons's *American Cookery* (1796), also abound with recipes for barberry pickles and jams.

Virtually unknown to eighteenth-century householders like Simmons, açaí 'berries' come from an Amazonian palm tree (*Euterpe oleracea*). They are dark purple and yield a thick pulp with a flavour somewhat resembling a slightly bitter chocolate-covered blackberry, which is used in smoothies and granola bowls. Açaí has recently taken the world by storm, mostly with the help of charlatans making wild claims about the nutritional and beauty-enhancing properties of the fruit. However disingenuous these claims may be, açaí does traditionally provide a high proportion of subsistence to indigenous Amazonians, making up nearly half of the diet of some populations.

Another berry much relished by indigenous people (but relatively unknown outside its native range) is the honeyberry (*Lonicera caerulea*). Also called 'haskap', from the word *hasukappu* used by the indigenous Ainu people of Hokkaido in northern Japan, the edible blue honeysuckle also grows wild in the subalpine forests of New England, and throughout northern and eastern Europe, but the people of Hokkaido are the only producers of commercial haskap products. The fruits are dark blue and somewhat elongated. They can be used interchangeably with blueberries, and are ideally suited to pies, jams and wine.

The plant wasn't domesticated until the 1950s in Russia, where it is still grown commercially, and American cultivation originated in Oregon in the 1990s using Japanese seed. In Finland and Sweden, where the plant is called *sinikuusama* and *blåtry* respectively, it's still a rare wildling under protective conservation.

At the other end of the world grows an unimposing plant known as the miracle fruit (*Synsepalum dulcificum*). Red miracle fruit berries look fairly basic but are, in fact, a psychedelic adventure for the mouth. While mapping the coast of Ouidah, Benin, in 1725, French cartographer Chevalier des Marchais observed the local people chewing red berries before meals and noted their sweetening properties. 'A glass of vinegar will taste, to the person trying the experiment, like sweet wine; a lime will seem to have the flavour of a very ripe China orange,' reported one dazzled correspondent in 1819.[11] In 1852 botanist W. F. Daniell remarked in his paper 'The Miraculous Berry of Western Africa' that the fruit that locals called *assarbah* or *iahme* was 'endowed with similar dulcificant virtues' and that it 'could change the flavour of the most acid substances into a delicious sweetness'.[12] The potent sourness of the native diet of fermented porridges and bread gruels washed down with beer and palm wine was seemingly – miraculously – dissipated.

The lives and needs of berries around the world are as diverse as the people who enjoy them. The stories and fables that humans construct around the tiny fruits are just as myriad, and even more sumptuous.

2
Berry-lore

Berry-picking plays such an important role in the European cultural vernacular that it's no wonder the pastime has seeped into the European mythos as well. Berries have long held a place in superstitions, religion and folklore. They are small and round, and come in a variety of colours imbued with mythical significance.

The national epic known as the *Kalevala*, compiled in the nineteenth century from Karelian and Finnish oral folklore and mythology, describes the immaculate conception of the young virgin Marjatta, who was impregnated by a magical lingonberry that she ate. As outlined in the fiftieth Rune of the epic, the shamanistic hero Väinämöinen orders the baby boy killed by having his head smashed against a birch tree, 'Since the child is but an outcast / Born and cradled in a manger / Since the berry is his father.'[1] The sentient two-week-old berry-baby chastizes Väinämöinen for saying such a horrible thing, and is baptized the king of Karelia. The infant king may have had a lingonberry for a father, but at least he didn't smell of elderberries.

Berry Amulets

Besides having magical fertility powers, berries can also be good omens and good-luck charms. Holly's merry red berries have long been associated with winter holidays. Druids hung holly boughs in their homes to invite sylvan sprites to take shelter there, and Roman pagans sent gifts and holly to their friends during the December holiday Saturnalia. Early Christians frowned upon decorating the home with holly in winter because of the associations with paganism, but eventually had a conciliatory change of heart; the blood-hued berries were later said to symbolize Christ's suffering, and now holly-bedecked halls are par for the Christmastime course.

The symbolism of red berries as blood didn't originate with Christianity, however. Ancient Hawaiians sacrificed humans to many of their deities, but not to the fire and volcano goddess Pele; rather, she received red 'Ōhelo berries (a cranberry relative) as a holy offering. British scholars wrote in the early twentieth century that rowans, hollies and yews 'are credited with a peculiar power in different parts of Europe [on] account of their berries being red . . . children wear their berries as a protective necklet'.[2] Amulets crafted with red berries were used to connote sacrificial and ritual bleeding, and were therefore worn by women and children, who were preferred offerings in European human sacrifices dating back to at least the first century AD.

Other colourful berry symbols abound in history. Blackberry charms were once used in Devonshire to cure blackheads, requiring the afflicted to crawl beneath an arched bramble three times in the direction of the sun, from east to west. The Green River Tribe (Skopahmish) of the Pacific Northwest believed that when white snowberries were plentiful, the runs of dog (chum) salmon, whose eyes resemble snowberries, would follow suit.

It's not just in amulets that berries find their place; sometimes they are used as symbolic foods. Elderberry wine, wild berries and berry pies are the traditional foods of the harvest festival Lughnasadh, also known as Bilberry Sunday or the Gule of August, one of the four Gaelic seasonal festivals and one of eight Sabbaths in the Neopagan/Wiccan Wheel of the Year. According to eighteenth-century accounts, the feast originally included the blueberry's sister the bilberry, but modern observances in the northeastern and northwestern U.S. typically use blueberries and blackberries respectively.

Bramble Briar

In the UK and Ireland, where hundreds of species of brambles grow, blackberry-lore proliferates. The Phooka (Púca) of Irish tales were mischievous faerie-folk blamed for the sorry state of blackberries at the end of the season, and children were warned not to eat overripe blackberries. Some Celtic lore considered blackberries *fae* (fey) fruit, bringing bad luck to all they touched, and in West Sussex, it was once believed that eating a blackberry after Old Michaelmas Day (10 October) would result in death or disaster to the eater or her kinfolk before the year's end.

When the archangel Michael expelled Lucifer from heaven, so the story goes, the condemned landed in a thicket of blackberry brambles (which was also the fabled burning bush in the midst of which God is said to have appeared to Moses). Lucifer, having had injury added to insult, threw a tantrum in the blackberry bushes, spitting and screaming and stamping his feet to curse and ruin the innocently bystanding berries.

In the fifth century a basilica was erected in Rome to remember the archangel's act and Michaelmas Day was celebrated until the eighteenth century.

Today, Michaelmas Day is celebrated on 29 September to honour the archangel, and 'Old Michaelmas Day' – also known as 'Devil's Spit Day' – was moved to 10 October when England adopted the Gregorian Calendar in 1752. Folklore dictates that it is the last day blackberries should be picked (but frankly, any later and they'll have gone off or become fodder for the waxwings). A Michaelmas pie is made from the season's last blackberries; Irish custom dictates a ring or some other trinket be hidden inside, and the finder of the ring is assured a marriage will soon follow.

Folklorist Richard Folkard wrote in his 1884 *Plant Lore* that 'to dream of Raspberries betokens success, happiness in marriage, fidelity in a sweetheart, and good news from abroad.'[3] Raspberries are said to have given the Roman goddesses Juno and Minerva the rosiness in their cheeks, and the ancient Greeks connected raspberries to the story of Ida (or Ide), a nymph and nursemaid to the infant Zeus, who saved him from his father by hiding him in a cradle suspended between the heavens and earth. Because of Pliny the Elder's mentions of raspberry's origins on Mount Ida (which was named for Zeus' clever babyminder), raspberry's Latin name, *Rubus idaeus*, means 'red bush of Ida'.

Fairy Tales

In the nineteenth-century Finnish tale 'The Raspberry King', young sisters Aina and Lisa find a worm in their bowl of raspberries and return him to safety beneath a bush instead of squashing him, as the girls' older siblings insist. Realizing they have eaten all of the berries that were to provide the winter's preserves, they return to the forest to replenish their supply. Of course, they become lost in the wood, but the little worm reveals himself to be a powerful and benevolent fairy king who rewards the girls' kind deed with a safe return home and ten big baskets of raspberries.

Classic European fairy tales often employed berry-picking as a device for getting young women or children alone in the forest to be deceived or subject to violence. For example, in 'Hansel and Gretel', the evil stepmother sends the children out to pick strawberries to punish them for slacking on their chores, with the added intention of being rid of them once and for all. And in 'The Wicked Wolverine' (a story collected in 1904 by folklorist Andrew Lang), the wolverine convinces a young she-bear to come out of a tree with the promise of all the cranberries she can eat, and then stabs her in the heart when she relents.

Russian fairy tales, collected by Aleksander Afanasyev in the mid-nineteenth century, were especially wont to use berries to move plots along. In one tale called 'The Bad Wife', a beleaguered husband tricks his browbeating harpy of a wife into falling into a pit behind a currant bush by using reverse psychology, convincing her to go and pick the berries. In the Russian fairy tale 'Snow White and the Fox', our protagonist becomes lost while picking berries with her friends and, presuming the worst, scrambles up a tree to cry about having been abandoned by her cruel friends. Snow White is visited first by a bear, and then a wolf, both of whom ask her to come down from the tree where she is crying and hiding, but she refuses out of fear of being eaten. A fox happens by, convinces her to come down and takes her home; he is repaid by Snow White's grandparents with a chicken . . . and then they sic their dog on him.

In a 1900s illustration to the Russian folk tale 'The Miraculous Pipe', Alionushka and her brother Ivanushka go picking berries for their mother, but only one of them returns.

In another Russian tale, 'The Miraculous Pipe', a priest's daughter named Alionushka wants to go and pick berries. Her mother makes her take her little brother Ivanushka along, and decides to make it 'interesting' by declaring that whoever gets the most berries will be rewarded with red slippers. Alionushka covets the slippers, but keeps eating the berries while her brother dutifully puts his in the basket he carries. By the end of the day, Alionushka has nothing and her obedient brother has a full basket of berries. Jealous, and really wanting those slippers, Alionushka slits Ivanushka's throat and buries him, returning home with his berries. (By the end of the long and circuitous tale, her ghastly crime is discovered thanks to a reed pipe possessed by her brother's talking ghost, and she is banished by her family.)

In one of the German tales collected by the Brothers Grimm, 'The Three Sisters', Marie, the youngest and prettiest of the three sisters, catches the eye of a local prince. She is sent out to pick strawberries by her jealous sisters, and their maid (a witch in disguise, naturally) sneaks back home, ditching Marie in the woods to die alone.

Of course, sometimes the berries themselves are central to the story. In the nineteenth-century Irish fairy tale 'The Fairy Tree of Dooros', fairies are said to feast on little rowan-like red berries that grow in fairyland. The fairy-berries

> are sweeter than any fruit that grows here in this world, and if an old man, bent and grey, ate one of them, he became young and active and strong again; and if an old woman, withered and wrinkled, ate one of them, she became young and bright and fair; and if a little maiden who was not handsome ate of them, she became lovelier than the flower of beauty.[4]

Such powerful berries must be closely guarded from greedy humans, and the fairies had to promise the fairy-monarchy not to bring any out of the fairy world into the Dooros Wood. (Predictably, one fairy accidentally does, and there is hell to pay. Giants, talking robins and endangered children feature prominently, but in the end, goodness prevails.)

Modern storytelling media pay homage to historic berry-magic, too. In the fifth (2014) edition of the longstanding fantasy role-playing game *Dungeons and Dragons*, the spell called 'Goodberry' is used by Druid character players to transmute magical energy into ordinary berries, rendering each berry as nourishing as a whole day's meals, and restoring one hit point per berry consumed. This harkens back to an ancient Celtic numerological belief that three berries from a certain magical tree make a man young, while one berry serves to sate the appetite as much as nine meals would.

It's Witchcraft

Medieval and early modern Europe were well supplied with Christian adaptations of ancient tales, and they still revealed a fascination with plant-based lore. Witches could be helpful or malevolent depending on the plants they used, but to Christians of the late Middle Ages and beyond, even helpful or 'white' witches were considered heretics. It didn't matter that she used her knowledge of herbs to heal; there was nothing more dreaded during the early modern period than a clever woman.

Though witches were feared and blamed for poisonings, most of them were simply guilty of enjoying a good psychedelic experience. During the witch trial of one fourteenth-century Irish woman, Dame Alice Kyteler, it was claimed that she had used berry-based ointments for flying on broomsticks. Today, she is remembered for having been the first woman tried and executed for being a witch. A few centuries later, recipes for witches' flying ointments regularly included nightshade berries (some also contained soot, bat's blood and baby's fat), but any sensation of flying was likely derived

Goya

Linda maestra!

Two witches on a broomstick, from Francisco Goya's *Los Caprichos* (1799). A witch's sensation of flying on a broomstick has been attributed to the psychotropic effects of nightshade berries.

Mandrake, from a medical-herbal manuscript of *c.* 1390. Mandrake berries, a powerful part of the witches' arsenal, simultaneously induce sleep and excite venereal fervour.

from the psychotropic effects of the nightshade and the other poisonous plants mixed in. University of Göttingen philologist Erich-Will Peuckert revealed in a 1960 interview that he and some friends had tried out a flying ointment recipe from the sixteenth-century book *Matica naturis* (substituting pork lard for the baby's fat); they passed out for twenty hours, and each experienced similar heavy metal nightmares.

Mandrake, also a member of the nightshade family, was another powerful member of the witches' arsenal. Mandrake berries somehow simultaneously induce sleep and excite venereal fervour; likewise, mild poisoning from nightshade purportedly causes one to fall into a deep sleep with the bonus of erotic lucid dreaming. These effects are almost certainly behind the accounts of witches claiming to have had sexual encounters with incubi or succubi.

According to Maud Grieve's *A Modern Herbal* (1931), nightshade 'belongs to the devil who goes about trimming and tending it in his leisure, and can only be diverted from its care on one night in the year, that is on Walpurgis, when he is preparing for the witches' Sabbath'.[5] Another nightshade, belladonna, gets its name (meaning 'beautiful woman'), from an old superstition that the plant is inhabited by the spirit of 'an enchantress of exceeding loveliness, whom it is dangerous to look upon'.[6] Another reason is that Italian women dripped its juice into their eyes to dilate their pupils, which conveys an appearance of sexual arousal.

Priests in Africa and India also sometimes employed berries in their trials by ordeal. Anthropologists in nineteenth-century Sierra Leone observed a practice which bears a strong resemblance to the pre-Christian Jewish 'ordeal of the bitter waters'. A woman suspected of adultery was given a drink of red water infused with poisonous berries (such as those from the syringa tree or Persian lilac), while uttering a prayer that she should be poisoned if she were guilty; if she were innocent, however, she could still die from the poison. The very accusation of adultery could be a death sentence.

Portents of Death and Doom

Berries were sometimes themselves symbols of death or bad omens. Nightshade was sometimes called death's herb, based on the belief that the berry induced a deathlike sleep; its old name dwale comes from the Dutch name *dvale*, meaning a trance or dead-sleep. Blackberries have a funereal association, insofar as blackberry vines were planted on fresh graves in village churchyards in order to prevent erosion of the freshly turned soil. A reverend of seventeenth-century England, Jeremy Taylor, wrote that 'the summer gives green turf and brambles to bind our graves.'[7]

'To dream of passing through places covered with brambles portends troubles,' warned Richard Folkard in *Plant Lore*.[8] 'If they prick you, secret enemies will do you an injury with your friends; if they draw blood, expect heavy losses in trade.'[9] However, Folkard notes that if one passes through the dream-brambles unharmed, the dreamer shall triumph over his enemies.

In German legends, strawberries symbolize dead children; likewise, if a mother of a dead child eats strawberries on St John's (Midsummer's) Eve, the Virgin Mary, who is said to rule the fruit as a symbol of righteousness, will banish her baby's soul from heaven.[10] In the old English ballad 'Babes in the Wood', robin redbreasts hide the bodies of two dead children under strawberry leaves.

> And when they were dead
> The robins so red
> Brought strawberry-leaves,
> And over them spread.[11]

Elder: Fairy-tree

Romani people called the elderberry *yakori bengeskro*, or devil's eye, and German folklore associates it with sorcery. Elder trees were considered a bad omen in old England, and there

Various tellings of 'Babes in the Wood' depict the dead children beneath berry bushes or leaves. In Randolph Caldecott's 1887 illustration the children are found beneath a blackberry bush.

IN ONE ANOTHER'S ARMS THEY DYED.

was once a Danish belief that if elder wood were used for building a cradle, evil would befall the baby. Conversely, Czechoslovakian Jews believed that if an elder twig sprouted when planted on a grave, that meant the soul of the deceased was happy. Elder trees have a long association with witchcraft and folklore, and for every baleful warning about the evil that lies inside them, there are dozens more extolling their beneficent magical powers.

Elder went by many pagan names: Dame Elder, *Hylde Moer* ('Elder Mother' in Danish), Old Lady and *Frau Holle* or *Frau Holda*. In English and Scandinavian tales, Elder Mother is a guardian-being, and cutting down an elder tree was once considered bad luck. Elder Mother would be angrily released to exact her revenge on the axeman unless he whispered the prayer, 'Owd Gal, give me some of thy wood an oi will give thee some of moine when I graws inter a tree.'[12] In ancient

Germanic folklore, Holda was an analogue to the goddess Perchta; as such, she appeared as both the haggard Dark Grandmother to whom dead babies are sent, and as the beautiful White Mother who brings snow in the winter with the shaking of her bedding.

Elder plays an important role in American applications of Germanic folklore as well, such as in powwow (also known

Frau Holle, the German depiction of Elder Mother, from an 1880s edition of the fairy tale 'Goldmarie and Pechmarie'.

as *Braucherei* in the *Deitsch* language), a type of American folk magic practised by the Pennsylvania Dutch. Powwow originated in pre-Christian German superstitions, and hints of old pagan beliefs peek through its religio-magical healing practices. Therefore we see the use of elder in the powwow pharmacopoeia because of the ancient beliefs in the tree's spiritual powers as well as the practical and demonstrable soothing benefits of the berry's syrup.

Wiccans believe that elderberries grant invisibility and second sight; that they cure the bites of mad dogs; and that they give the user eternal youth. Drinking elderberry wine is considered to be a gateway to the fairy world, and sprinkling a fire with elderberries invites fairies to one's gathering.

Rowan: The Quicken-tree

The Norse thunder-god Thor crossed the river Vimur while travelling through Jotunheim, the land of the Frost Giants. The giantess Gjalp straddled the river as the waters flowed from her body, causing the river to rise and roil violently. Thor grabbed onto a rowan growing on the streambank and scrambled out, earning the tree the name 'Thor's salvation'. In the Icelandic saga *Grettir's Ævikviða* (an epic poem of medieval Scandinavia) rowan is also called by the name *þórbjǫrg*, meaning 'saving Thor'.

Known as the rune-tree, rowan is featured in scores of northern European myths, and was of particular importance in Norse and Gaelic legends, representing a merging of the histories and mythologies of the two peoples. Rowan trees were considered to be especially effective at preventing the evil influences of witches and the evil eye, and were used in Scottish amulets for this purpose.

Depiction of Thor crossing the river Vimur, grasping a rowan branch, 1900s. The tree is known as 'Thor's salvation'.

The supernatural warrior-wizards of Irish mythology known as the Tuatha De' Danaan pinned down the freshly dead with rowan-wood spikes to prevent them from becoming vampires. The classical Gaelic legend 'The Pursuit of Diarmuid and Gráinne', which very likely inspired 'The Fairy-tree of Dooros', tells of the quicken-tree of Dubhros, which bore magical berries. 'There is in every berry the exhilaration of wine, and the satisfying of old mead, and whoever shall eat three berries of them, has he completed a hundred years, he will return to the age of thirty years.'[13] Left to guard them was a hideous giant named Searbhan who was so fierce that the entire warrior class, the Fianna, were terrified even to hunt nearby. The story's dutiful hero, Diarmuid O'Duibhne, slayed Searbhan with his own club because Diarmuid's pregnant wife Gráinne was having an insatiable craving for the berries.

All Around the Mulberry Bush

Though it's because of their association with silk moths rather than their being a source of fruit to humans, mulberry trees are central to ancient Chinese mythology. The Leaning Mulberry Tree (*Fu-Sang*) is the world-tree of Chinese solar myth that directs the rising and setting of the sun. According to the *Huai Nan Zi* (*c.* second century BC), it was within mulberry forests that the gods communicated with humans, and where people offered their sacrifices and prayed for rain. The Son of Heaven prohibited any forester from cutting down *Fu Sang* trees.

Other tales, which straddle history and myth, tell of the importance of mulberry. Said to have been discovered as an infant after his mother was transformed into a hollow mulberry tree, Yi Yin was a hero of early Chinese writings. He is said to have been chef to the king Tang of Shang, gifted with powers granted from bearing the cooking vessel of the gods.

Nicolas Poussin, *Stormy Landscape with Pyramus and Thisbe*, 1651, oil on canvas.

It may be that Yi Yin, who did live in the fourteenth century BC, was actually found abandoned as an infant, his tale being one of a low-born person rising to high status through his deeds and talents. In this case, the hollow mulberry tree is symbolic of his humble origins.

The Japanese, too, believe that mulberry trees hold sacred powers which make the groves repellent to lightning. Akin to saying 'knock on wood', Japanese superstition compels them to mumble *kuwabara kuwabara* (mulberry plantation) for good luck, or more specifically, during thunderstorms to trick the thunder god into avoiding them.

The purple colour of mulberries was said to have come from the blood of two ill-fated lovers in Ovid's *Metamorphosis*. Two young sweethearts, Thisbe and Pyramus, are forbidden by their families from marrying, so they plan a rendezvous under the mulberry tree near the tomb of Ninus. Thisbe arrives first, but encounters a lioness and flees for her life. Pyramus arrives to see the lioness' tracks in the mud and a piece of Thisbe's dress, torn during her escape. Distraught, Pyramus kills himself with his own sword and bleeds onto the white mulberries lying on the ground. Feeling the coast must by now be clear, Thisbe emerges from her hiding place a moment later and returns to the tree to find her dear Pyramus bleeding out. She cries out in anguish, then picks up her lover's sword and impales herself through the heart, her blood joining Pyramus' to stain the mulberries. The mulberry was purple thereafter. (Coincidentally, the Latin name for mulberry, *morus*, means 'foolish' – a loan-word from the Greek *moron* that could be used to describe someone who jumps to Pyramus' drastic conclusions.)

Native American Folktales

Like all gathering tasks of yore, berry-picking was typically women's work, and Native American myths sometimes utilize berry-picking in a way similar to European fairy tales, providing an excuse for women to be alone in the woods. In one creation myth from the Pacific Northwest, the Origin of the Thunder Bird, a giantess named Quoots-hooi was picking berries when she came upon the nest of the Thunder Bird, full of eggs. She rolled one of the eggs down a mountain and it turned into a person; she rolled each of the other eggs down the mountainside, creating all of the Chehalis tribe. In other myths told by native people throughout the region, all of mankind was created by the gods Silver Fox and Coyote whittling humans out of serviceberry wood.

In one tale shared among the Coast Salish people of British Columbia, Blue-Jay gambles with the ghosts in the Land of the Dead, and is chagrined to find that the basket he holds is filled not with berries, but with angry bees.

The Clackamas Chinook people of northwestern Oregon passed on a tale at the beginning of each berry season. In the stories, the deity Coyote would pass by different berry bushes, whereupon each species of berry would declare, 'I'm going to stab you, Coyote!' Coyote would then pluck each berry and eat it, declaring it suitable for humans. In other North American regions, berries are used in myths to similar end, to convey the arrival of summer. Observations of Pacific Northwest people's relationships with berries and other food plants are consistent with those made by other ethnologists of other American tribes. Berries are considered to be divine gifts from the gods, and remembering to thank the gods for these gifts ensured a happy place in the afterlife.

Seneca people of the northeastern United States pay homage to strawberries as a harbinger of spring and rebirth, and the Cherokee of the southeastern United States tell a myth wherein strawberries reunite the first man with his estranged wife. Shortly after the creation of the woman, the couple began to argue, until finally the wife had had enough and left him. The man was pretty torn up about it, and the sun goddess Unelanuhi felt sorry for him and offered to help. To lure the wife back, Unelanuhi first made a patch of huckleberries sprout along the wife's path, but she passed them by, uninterested. Other berry bushes appeared, one after another, but none caught the woman's eye. Finally, Unelanuhi created strawberries, which the woman picked and ate with relish. The berries rekindled her affections for her husband; she collected handfuls to bring to him, and they lived happily ever after. The strawberries remained on earth as a symbol of female sensual pleasure.

The Ojibwa people of the Lake Superior area of Canada and the u.s. share a tale of mountain ash berries. The legend tells that hunters are struggling to find food when they discover many dead birds and small mammals lying in snowdrifts. Fearful that they will come to a similar fate, they begin to pray to the Great Manitou (Spirit), who hears their pleas. Manitou instructs them to take one drop of blood from each dead creature and to smear it on the tree most crucial to the survival of the people. The hunters choose the mountain ash, as their bows and arrows are hewn from the wood of that tree. The next morning, every mountain ash tree that has been smeared with blood is bearing fruit, and the small animals are all perched in the trees and eating the berries. (The tale doesn't spell it out here, but presumably the hunters rain down annihilation on the animals and provide meat, rather than berries, to their village.) The hunters give thanks with a happy dance, and Manitou promises that whenever they expect a harsh winter, the tree will provide.

The Cree, who lived very close to the Ojibwa, ate berries at every ceremony. Some ceremonies, such as one made in offering to the Bear Spirit, imbued sacred medicine bundles (cloth or skins wrapped around symbolic objects) with powers that were activated by eating berries at the ceremony's conclusion. At other times, such as following a successful bear hunt, shrines prepared in honour of the Bear Spirit were given bowls of berries as offerings. In one tale, the ripening of the berries triggers a pivotal event: the meeting between Great Bear and his clever and fearless adversary Pot-belly.

For millennia, people have intertwined their traditional beliefs with berries, and have even integrated them into their spiritual rituals. The act of picking and eating wild berries has come to underpin the very cultural identity of many of the world's nations. Enjoying berries in the temple of nature is, in the views of some, every person's right.

3
Picking and Growing

Of all the plant foods controlled by humans, berries have always maintained friendly relations with their country cousins. Wild berries are as beloved as tame ones. 'Many of the wild berries are seedlings from cultivated varieties,' noted an American horticulturist in 1880, 'and a few wild plants have been selected which may prove of value to small fruit cultivators.'[1] While blackberry breeders work diligently to create newer, bigger, juicier varieties, wild blackberries still make up a significant portion of the global harvest; nearly 15,000 tonnes of wild blackberries were harvested in 2005 alone. People seem to love picking berries just as much as they love eating them.

Berries have often been the first plant foods that nomadic people have eaten to survive when they have arrived to a new area. Although many are poisonous, berries are immediately recognizable as possible food. The Dutch colonizing South Africa found berries to eat while waiting for their crops to grow, for example, while the native Khoisan and Herero people already living in the region supplemented their game-heavy diet with berries found around the bush.

Wild berries from the Innoko National Wildlife Refuge, Alaska.

Land Down Under

The people of Oceania (Australia, Tasmania and New Zealand, plus Polynesia and Micronesia) have utilized various berries throughout their respective histories. Nineteenth-century botanist Joseph Hooker wrote with dismay that the flora of the island of Tasmania was merely 'eatable', but 'not fit to eat'.[2] Earlier European explorers had come to similar conclusions, finding that the appleberry was 'almost the only eatable fruit that grows spontaneously in that country'.[3] The inhabitants of the region were wont to disagree, as they incorporated many fruits into their native diet, and later botanists of Australia even found some of the berries to be pleasant.

It might be easy to dismiss Australia as a parched land of red desert sands and eucalyptus trees, but many berries thrive there: wild cape gooseberry (aka ground cherry), Indian mulberry (also a famine food in some Polynesian cultures), riberry (aka lilly pilly), appleberries, a native cranberry (*Astroloma humi-fusum*, related to *Vaccinium* spp.) and various brambles all make up a part of the traditional aboriginal diet. 'Bush tucker', or wild food, has enjoyed a surge in popularity with non-indigenous people of Oceania, similar to how foraged ingredients are gaining cachet in fine dining restaurants across Europe and North America.

Indigenous Americans

From springtime strawberries to the huckleberries at summer's end, Native Americans relied on berries for a fresh source of vitamins as well as for replenishing their emptied winter caches; berries also delineated the spring and summer months for the people, as a sort of living calendar.

Unlike some of the unfamiliar foods of the native people, European Americans found wild berries to be just as delectable as native people did. 'The kinds best known are the black-berry, strawberry, huckleberry, salmon-berry, sallal, Oregon

Appleberry is a source of bush tucker for indigenous Australians.

Mandan Native American women gathering buffalo berries, c. 1908.

grape, squawberry, and others,' wrote historian Herbert Lang in 1885, but for native people, the berries were much more than a summertime treat.[4]

During the late summer, indigenous women throughout North America gathered berries in droves, both for eating fresh off the bush during bountiful times and, more importantly, for drying and storing. Huckleberry season was treated as a summertime social holiday in the mountains before the fishing and hunting season arrived, with its frenetic pace requiring all hands on deck. In 1615 explorer Samuel de Champlain noted Algonquin women in what is today eastern Ontario, Canada, picking huckleberries and drying them for the winter. Fresh berries could be dried simply as raisins are, or mashed into fat cakes weighing 4–7 kg (10–15 lb) each by packing the dried fruits with fat. Dried berries were also mixed with smoked meats, fish and suet into the travel rations known as pemmican.

The First Fruits festival of Pacific Northwest peoples honoured berries with a feast held at the beginning of the berry season. Berry-picking could not begin until the ceremony was completed. Feasts were also held to celebrate a girl's first berry harvest as a contributing member of her family – an important rite of passage for young women (though women were not allowed to pick berries if they were menstruating). Special berry vessels were prepared as well: in the Pacific Northwest these could be Klickitat baskets woven from beargrass and western red cedar bark, or in the Great Plains they might be cylindrical baskets made of birch bark.

Berries were so important to people of the Pacific Northwest that they were integral to the First Salmon Festival, another sacred annual ritual. A salmonberry was placed in the mouth of the first salmon caught before the salmon fishing could begin in earnest. The juicy-orange salmonberry would go on to be loved by others as well, even though its persistent carpels could be a bit tiresome. 'They would be the best berry that grows if they only shaved,' one nineteenth-century camper lamented of the hirsute berry.[5]

Before the Second World War, indigenous and white people in the Pacific Northwest picked huckleberries in large camps for home use and for commercial sale. The gradual adoption of white people's practice of canning berries rather than drying them in situ contributed to the decline of Native Americans' social tradition of berry-picking on public lands.[6]

Sami

Lingonberries, bilberries and several species of bramble have been a staple food to the Sami, indigenous Finno-Ugric people of Sápmi (also known as Lapplanders). Because of the general lack of vegetables in the Arctic, berries provide much-needed minerals to a diet primarily consisting of fish and reindeer meat. Overwhelmingly, their diet resembles that of the northern and boreal tribes of Native Americans.

During his botanical visits through the region, Linnaeus noted with some surprise that the Sami preferred eating cloudberries with reindeer milk over sugary cakes. Cloudberries – a small orange-fruited blackberry variety – are called *multe* in Norway, or *lakka* in Finland. As a traditional food, cloudberries are of particular cultural significance to Finland, where they appear on the 2-euro coin.

Hobby Picking

Some people picked berries to contribute not just to their family stores, but to the family coffers as well, selling or trading surplus for other goods. In his poem 'Blueberries' (1915), Robert Frost wrote fondly of his time spent picking wild berries with his aunt and uncle when he was a child.

Outside Europe, the written accounts of campers provide a snapshot of hobby berry-picking during a time when recreational camping was gaining interest in the UK in the latter

Inuit berry-pickers in Nome, Alaska, in the early 1900s.

part of the nineteenth century. This came just a few decades after Overlanders travelling across the American West on the Oregon Trail brought a yen for wild berries to the Pacific Coast. Emigrants supplemented their diets with berries picked along the way, sweetening the hard journey with the occasional pie, and with berry-picking's brief reprieve from the monotony of the dusty trail.

On the other side of the pond, people were similarly keen on picking berries. Charles Dickens, too, waxed nostalgic for his times spent on berry forays:

> How bountifully Nature had spread her table in that wild country all round! As far as the eye could reach lay the ripe red berries, growing in such abundance that the leaves of the plants were hardly to be seen for the fruit, and you could gather a quart without moving from where you stood, off the little low bushes barely two

and a half feet high. In fact they grew so low that you could sit down and fill your pail, and many of us did, picking meantime, children's fashion, 'two in the mouth and one in the basket.' And these berries had certainly a most delicious flavour; they beat the common garden raspberry in that, if not in size.[7]

His party also picked wild currants, cherries, and plums, 'But the raspberry was certainly the best of the wild fruits.'[8]

Freedom to Roam ('Everyman's Right')

As mentioned in the previous chapter, the indigenous Japanese people known as the Ainu have long harvested *hasu-kappu* (haskap; honeyberries or blue honeysuckle). This relates to an important aspect of Japanese culinary heritage: the springtime collection of *sansai*, 'mountain vegetables', and the preparation of *shun* (seasonal) food. Permits are typically required for non-municipal residents to harvest wild foods, but the policy is evidently never enforced. For the Japanese residents, there is no law providing for one's free access to the wilds and their products, but no one would be hassled for walking in the woods and picking wild raspberries.

Across northern Europe (particularly Nordic and Baltic countries), 'Everyman's Rights' or freedom-to-roam laws grant unfettered access to wild lands and the berries that grow within them. Unless they're growing in obviously cultivated fields, berries and other forest products are all fair game in countries with these laws. Families go to the woods to collect berries together and enjoy some fresh air. The scope of the Finnish laws is the broadest, entitling anyone living or staying in Finland to enjoy nearly complete freedom, regardless of land ownership, as long as the land and its other occupants are treated respectfully. With a few etiquette-based exceptions that prevent squatting or lingering too close to occupied homes, accessing lands for hiking, skiing and overnight camping is a fundamental right; picking flowers, mushrooms and berries is a protected liberty in Finland, Sweden, Norway, Iceland, Estonia, Lithuania and Latvia. To Scots, wandering the heath and *stravaiging* for *blaeberries* is a centuries-old right.

The berry-picking freedom enjoyed by the Finnish is not without its problems, however; the primary downside is that some commercial fruit companies, seizing on the Japanese, Chinese and South Korean fervour for wild Nordic bilberries, lingonberries and cloudberries, have taken to exploiting the liberal laws. During Southeast Asia's summer monsoon season (which coincides with Nordic berry season), thousands of seasonal labourers migrate from Thailand to earn money harvesting the wild berries from the boreal forests of Sweden and Finland. The fruit companies earn healthy profits, but the locals don't always share these benefits.

Unlike in Finland, in Norway cloudberries are protected as an integral part of the Sami culinary heritage, but anyone is allowed to eat the berries one encounters in the field (as long as one isn't hopping fences to access them). Locals are allowed to pick as long as they display proper berry-picking manners: don't crash someone else's patch, leave the unripe berries for others and use one's own legs (not ATVs or bikes) to get to the patches. One blogger's guide to picking cloudberries warns of the consequences of disregarding this etiquette: 'The culprits are dealt with the only way Norwegians know how.'[9] (Anyone who's watched an episode of *Vikings* understands what this might mean.)

Cape gooseberries, also known as goldenberries, are a weedy Peru native that have been in passive cultivation for centuries.

Cultivation, Domestication and Breeding

Some berries make the transition from wild to cultivated in rather minor ways, such as the weedy goldenberry (also called cape gooseberry or ground cherry) of Peru, gathered from the wild by snacking children. The plant volunteers in Andean gardens, and is known to pioneer disturbed waste areas. It's only recently begun appearing in farmer's markets and better-stocked produce stands outside South America, where the fruit is still mostly treated as a novelty.

Half-wild plants such as the goldenberry can easily make the transition to intentional cultivation, but nowadays we humans will rarely make the effort unless the fruit makes it worth our while; specifically, if it can withstand shipping and fetch a good price. For centuries, local consumption was the only reason for cultivation.

Early Domestication and Breeding

While the berry-loving nations of Europe have satisfied their appetites on wild berries, the u.s. has dominated in breeding programmes. The state of Oregon has been a leader in cane-berry breeding for more than a century, and this is thanks in large part to the sheer variety of esculent wild blackberries to provide breeders the necessary germ plasm. 'The testimony of travelers and botanists shows, beyond cavil, that there is no country in the known world where wild berries are so common as in Oregon,' wrote Herbert Lang (perhaps somewhat hyperbolically) in 1885.[10]

> In the woods and prairies of this part of the State, no less than eighteen varieties of edible berries, some of them equal in flavour to cultivated sorts, exist, abundant, large and delicious, mostly unknown or little appreciated by man.[11]

Cloudberries are of significant cultural importance to Scandinavians.

That may have been true at the time it was written, but those are also fighting words to people hailing from the state of Maine, where wild blueberries still reign supreme.

Although European berries were commercially grown in the U.S. in the early 1800s, complaints soon emerged of blackberry and strawberry cultivars' inferior flavour compared to the wild cousins. Even though wild berries seldom reach the impressive size of the domesticated berries, their flavour is often superior to the fat and juicy ones; 'there are no "oh! oh's!" and nothing is said about "big berries,"' wrote one Canadian horticulturist in 1884.[12] It would appear that, at least with berries, size doesn't always matter.

Of all the berries in the world, overall it has been a relatively small selection of strawberries, caneberries and blueberry kin that have received the plant breeder's helping hand, though huckleberries have been notoriously difficult to civilize. Perhaps it's for this tendency of huckleberries to prefer living out in the sticks that fictional country bumpkins Huckleberry Finn and Huckleberry Hound were so named.

Pliny the Elder gave only passing mention to berries, and aside from occasional accounts of medicinal uses, botanists of ancient Greece largely overlooked berries because they weren't agricultural crops. By the fourteenth century, however, this changed; the French began transplanting wild strawberry plants from the forest into their own garden plots, utterly simplifying their future berry-picking.

The small round berries were both gastronomically and aesthetically pleasing, and medieval monks began featuring them in their illuminated manuscripts. 'The [strawberry] plants may form the entire decoration as in our frontispiece, or a single plant may be placed in an important spot, at the feet of the Madonna or in the Child's hand,' botanist George Darrow explains in his 1966 monograph on the berry.[13] The French

A variety of caneberries growing on a farm in Oregon.

king Charles V was a generous patron of these miniaturists, and also hired a gardener to tend 12,000 strawberry plants within his Royal Gardens.

By the mid-1800s, guidebooks such as Richard Gay Pardee's *Complete Manual for the Cultivation of the Strawberry; With a Description of the Best Varieties, Also, Notices of the Raspberry, Blackberry, Gooseberry, and Grape* (1854) were being published for lay gardeners as well as professional growers, following several years of trial and error. 'It is pleasant to know that so many intelligent cultivators are now turning their attention to the production of these fine fruits,' Pardee wrote optimistically.[14]

Blackberries were always a weedy friend growing in hedgerows and along fence lines across the North American, British and Eurasian countrysides, and then in the mid- to late nineteenth century, it occurred to American horticulturists to begin selecting bigger and more flavourful berries for breeding. In 1881 California judge and amateur plant breeder James H. Logan accidentally invented the loganberry when he planted two blackberries (likely 'Aughinbaugh' and 'Texas

Miniature of Pilate from a French Book of Hours (*c.* 1426–38) depicting strawberry plants. Artworks like this one inspired Charles v to instruct his gardeners to plant 12,000 strawberry plants.

Wild woodland strawberries.

Early') next to an old-growth 'Red Antwerp' raspberry vine in his backyard. The three plants flowered at the same time and enjoyed a botanical ménage à trois, and then Logan planted the seeds from the resulting fruit. Of the fifty seedlings produced, one was noticeably robust; he named this berry after himself (the loganberry), and the rest of the seedlings produced the longest berries that had yet been grown, which were dubbed the Mammoth.

The loganberry was introduced to the American east coast about fifteen years later, and to Europe soon after that. It's been used as a parent plant to numerous successful cultivars, including the California-bred boysenberry and the olallieberry, which was produced at Oregon State University and later bred with Chehalem berry to produce the marionberry. Loganberries are grown throughout North America and the UK, but its descendants have parted ways; olallieberries are now primarily grown in California, while marionberries are mainly grown in Oregon and boysenberries in New Zealand.

Luther Burbank

While Judge Logan was messing around in his backyard in the 1880s, the prolific botanist and plant breeder Luther Burbank had been blowing minds with the hundreds of varieties of plants he had been inventing – using what appeared to be nothing more than intuition and good vibes. He invented the Russet potato with the sole intent of solving the Irish potato famine. He came up with the freestone July Elberta peach and elephant garlic, and many more food plants, all without recording notes on his work. The scientific method just wasn't his cup of tea. He was happier out in the garden.

Luther Burbank's 'white blackberry'.

Luther Burbank, American agriculturalist and developer of the 'white blackberry' in 1910.

In 1905 Burbank wrote that the laws of heredity merely gave man a tool for 'guiding and molding the creative forces of nature'. His discoveries, he argued, were merely iterations of the 'strange freak' that had always resided in the plant's ancestry; by teasing out these intricate threads from the tapestry of life, one is provided with 'a more general knowledge that all motion, all life, all force, all so-called matter are following the same law of heredity'.[15]

Although he was criticized by scientists for his lack of methodical rigour (and modern weed managers have cursed his introduction of the highly invasive and exceedingly thorny 'prolific Himalaya' blackberry to the American West), Burbank was beloved by Americans. He even had his own fan club, the Luther Burbank Society, which published a bulletin and Burbank's twelve-volume set of books describing his work.

Besides, his discoveries weren't just botanical curiosities; they helped people. By the 1910s Burbank had finally accomplished a thornless blackberry variety after thirty years of trying, and had turned his attention to breeding one that would also bear high-quality fruit. 'When any visitor who has the recollection of such souvenirs visits my garden and sees mammoth clusters of beautiful blackberries growing on vines as smooth as pussy willows, the impression gained is both vivid and lasting that here is a plant improvement of a very notable order,' wrote Burbank in 1914.

By the time Burbank died in 1926, he had invented more than eight hundred new plant varieties; that same year, a mutant called 'Thornless Evergreen' was discovered in the wild in Oregon and was quickly adopted for cultivation. However, as Burbank had previously noted, the mutant form (a genetic chimera) often reverts back to being thorny if it is damaged, so breeding efforts soon began to use the variety for genetic material. Eventually a totally thornless loganberry was developed in 1933. Nowadays, thornless or semi-erect varieties are still something of an anomaly for home gardeners, but they're doubtless a welcome sight to berry-pickers.

Little Hands, Big Work

'Pick-your-own' or 'U-pick' berry farms have offered urbanites a convenient opportunity to harvest the freshest berries at a reduced price, closely following the widespread production of berries for markets. Advertisements for pick-your-own berries began to appear in American newspapers

Cranberry pickers in a flooded bog in New Jersey, 1938.

and magazines in the early 1910s. 'Save expense by gathering your berries,' the ads suggest.[16]

Besides apples, berries are the most common U-pick crop. Fresh berries don't ship well, and combined with the labour-intensiveness of their harvest, berries lend themselves well to a pick-your-own system. For the latter reason, child labour has also been favoured for berry-picking. Children of the Baby Boomer era could always easily secure summer work picking berries in nearby fields, and school buses would cart youngsters out en masse to earn a little spending cash or to help out with family finances.

The precedent had been set several decades earlier, when slave labour evaporated following the American Civil War. American author (and abolitionist) Lydia Maria Child wrote

Five-year-old Alberta McNabb, in her third season of berry-picking, Delaware, 1910. She worked from sunup to sundown.

in 1829 that sending one's children out to pick a few pints of berries for the market was good for them, but written mentions of hiring children for one's workforce appear in gardening guides and magazines about a decade after the war's end. 'It is a common notion that anybody, even a child, can pick strawberries,' stated *American Agriculturist* in 1877, while warning that children are not famous for their attention to detail and that 'skilled labour' was required if the crop were to make it past the shipping process intact.[17] Quality control aside, it didn't take long for child labour to catch on as a preferred mode of berry harvesting.

Photographer Lewis Hine captured images of children picking berries (and performing other jobs) across America from 1908 to 1912, and was eventually hired by the National Child Labor Committee to document illegal child labour practices. One 1910 report from Philadelphia found that children – some as young as three years of age – comprised up to half of the labour force in some cranberry bogs in the northeastern u.s., sometimes weeks past the beginning of the school year. Although the most stringent of the child labour laws went on the books in the u.s. in 1938, several large commercial berry-growers have subsequently been cited for employing children as young as five years old, and as recently as 2016.

Driscoll's Takes the West

Commercial strawberry growing began in the Pajaro Valley of California in 1872, and twenty years later two brothers named Richard and Donald Driscoll immigrated from County Cork, Ireland, to get a piece of the action.[18] They formed their company in Watsonville, California, in 1904, and by 2016 it was employing a global team of 40,000 'Joy Makers' – agronomists, plant breeders, plant pathologists, entomologists and analysts.[19] Driscoll's is now the world's largest berry-grower.

Japanese farmers grew berries all over the western u.s. before the Second World War. Also located in Watsonville, Hiroshi Shikuma was another of America's most productive berry-growers, and the Sakuma Brothers near Seattle, Washington, have been growing berries since 1915. At the time it formed in 1917, the Central California Berry Grower

Association (CCBGA, which became Naturipe four decades later) was made up of half Japanese farmers.

The CCBGA funded berry research at the University of California at Berkeley until the Second World War, when the university made the short-sighted decision to redirect research into cotton-growing for the war effort. Ned Driscoll, a third-generation berry-farmer, created a private research institute, which allowed research to continue unabated during the war, but which also had the effect of monopolizing the science for the Driscolls, who had already begun patenting berries and growing their own proprietary varieties. After the unjust internment of Japanese American citizens during the war, Driscoll's invited the released prisoners to become sharecroppers in the company. They were the first American company to export strawberries to China, and still have the Asian market cornered. They also operate in northern Africa, the Middle East and throughout the EU.

In Mexico, where the majority of berries are produced today (most global berry companies, including Driscoll's, have ground operations there), more than 100,000 people are employed by berry-growers. Blueberries have done especially well there, particularly since most of the berry farms are located around a kilometre and a half above sea level where the climate is more temperate. Spain produces the second largest crop of berries in the world, though Italy is not far behind.

Knott's Berry Farm

Walter Knott and his wife Cordelia owned a berry farm in southern California called Knott's Berry Farm. In the late 1920s Walter Knott began working with George Darrow, a

Raspberries, from a California growers' guide (1910).

Knott's Berry Farm in Orange County, California.

u.s. Department of Agriculture plant-breeder (and afore-mentioned authority on strawberries) who had enlisted his help. Darrow had heard of an interesting new berry growing on a farm owned by a California grower named Rudolph Boysen, and soon he and Knott learned that Boysen had abandoned his new berry. The two men transplanted Boysen's berry back to Knott's farm and nursed it back to health. Soon, the 'boysenberry', as it came to be known, was one of the berries sold on Knott's Berry Farm, and the jams and pies that Cordelia made from the berries made the farm famous.

To accommodate the growing crowds, the Knotts soon added a restaurant to serve chicken dinners in 1934, on trend throughout the u.s. in the first half of the twentieth century. The restaurant was so popular that by 1940, Walter Knott had begun to construct a replica Wild West ghost town on the property to attract more visitors. By the late 1960s they had begun charging admission, and now Knott's Berry Farm, has forty rides in four different themed areas, and saw more than

3.8 million visitors in 2015. Their jam is still being sold today under the Smucker's brand.

Humans have spent centuries trying to master the ins and outs of a berry's genome – trying to civilize a fruit that some say is best left to the wilds. Fortunately, such time has also been spent mastering the dishes and drinks that highlight a berry's true talents.

4
Dishes and Drinks

Berries have long saved a hostess from having to come up with a clever finale to a summertime dinner party. (That is, of course, unless she was planning on carving intricate hop-flowers from gooseberries, as was the trend in the Georgian period.) No proper Victorian home would have been complete without a berry set consisting of a 'master' berry bowl and four to six individual bowls. In well-heeled households, the butler's pantry would also contain a berry spoon and three-tined (or sometimes two-tined) strawberry forks as standard items in the silver cabinet.

Having pretty china bowls and silver spoons relieved a housewife of having to do anything at all with the fruits, which was just as some preferred. Domestic expert Marion Harland warns in her *Common Sense in the Household* (1884) that the flavour and quality of berries are ruined by washing the delicate fruits; 'If they are so gritty as to require this process, keep them off the table.'[1] One should simply 'put them on the table in glass dishes, piling them high and lightly', with cream and powdered sugar for guests to add themselves.[2] 'It is not economical, perhaps,' she admitted, during a time when powdered sugar was a luxury not all homes could afford, 'but it is a healthful and pleasant style of serving them – I had almost said the only decent one.'[3]

Marion Harland could never have predicted the hellscape that is modern artificial 'berry' flavour, used in myriad products the world over to convey girlishness despite being the antithesis of wholesome simplicity. Found in everything today from vodka to body lotion, the organic compound furaneol is an alcohol naturally found in a variety of fruits, strawberries especially. Furaneol, and ethyl methylphenylglycidate (commonly known as 'strawberry aldehyde'), are used frequently by the flavour and perfume industries, perhaps in an allusion to Elizabethan poet Edmund Spenser's true love, whose 'goodly bosome' smelled daintily 'lyke a Strawberry bed'.[4]

Another innocent victim of modern food science, blue raspberry is a common flavour for fizzy drinks (sodas), syrups, sweets (candies) and even headaches; brainfreeze-inducing Sno-Kones have been flavoured with the lurid blue syrup since their invention in the late 1950s. In fact, artificial blue raspberry was given its hue specifically so the various berry flavours of frozen treats could be distinguished from one

Homemade jelly displayed at a roadside stand near Northampton, Massachusetts, in 1939.

Though a blue raspberry does occur in nature, it bears no resemblance in colour to the artificial blue raspberry flavouring found in so many products today.

another. There had already been questions about the safety of the dye being used for dark raspberry red (FD&C Red No. 2, later banned as a carcinogen). Changing the raspberry flavour to a different colour killed two birds with one stone. By the early 1970s Sno-Kone competitor ICEE had added a blue raspberry flavour as well.

Convenience store chain 7-Eleven debuted a blue raspberry Slurpee-flavoured doughnut in 2016 in honour of the week-long American television event known as 'Shark Week'. There was even a blue raspberry Slurpee-flavoured Chapstick lip balm introduced the same year. It turns out that 2016 was a banner year for blue raspberry.

Things were so much simpler before the blue mania. In 1973 the world's first flavoured lip gloss, Bonne Belle's Lip Smackers, was introduced to American markets with a strawberry flavour, and first kisses have never been sweeter.

Ancient Uses

Most early written records, such as those from Pliny the Elder, largely ignored berries as an esculent because they were merely common peasant fare gathered wild, not 'civilized' food worthy of the printed word. Besides, unlike dates and figs, most berries didn't grow especially well in the Mediterranean or the supposedly Fertile Crescent. Mulberries were commonly eaten throughout Mesopotamia and the Levant, however. The earliest known cookbook, *De re coquinaria* (Of Culinary Matters), purportedly by first-century gastronome Marcus Gavius Apicius and so also known as *Apicius*, includes a recipe for preserving mulberries in their own juice and wine, though the author warns that the mulberries must be watched 'all the time' to prevent their spoiling.[5] Ancient Egyptians included mulberries, along with *nabk* berries (*Ziziphus lotus*; a relative of jujube), among the dates, grapes and figs they ate; a dish of *nabk* was discovered among the funerary offerings left at the Saqqara necropolis site.

In the sixth century BC the Indian physician Sushruta recommended eating sour fruit such as amla (Indian gooseberry; *Phyllanthus emblica*). *Amla* means sour or acidic in Sanskrit, and, along with salt, sweet, bitter, astringent and pungent, is one of the six tastes in ancient Indian cooking – the taste that makes one's mouth water and increases appetite.

Barberries, or *zereshk*, have been an integral element of the Persian rice dishes *zereshk polow* and *morgh polow* for centuries, and barberry soup was listed on a seasonal menu as an appropriate summer food to be served at the Topkapı Palace in the fifteenth century. The seventeenth-century travelogue of Ottoman explorer Evliya Çelebi mentions mulberry pilaf, and four centuries earlier the poet Rumi purportedly enjoyed pilaf with currants.

On the other side of Europe, ancient Norse people ate wild berries as they found them, and very likely dried or pickled some for storage, similar to indigenous people across the Arctic. Archaeological evidence found in Denmark, Switzerland and England revealed a variety of berries were included in the diets of ancient Europeans.

In his 2015 *The Nordic Cook Book*, Magnus Nilsson writes that because of the lack of sugar in the Scandinavia of yore, preserves like jam were probably not made in average households. However, he also notes that some simple dishes, such as *rødgrød med fløde* (berries thickened with potato starch, served with cream), are among 'the most iconic and common'

A dish of spicy amla, or pickled Indian gooseberry.

Dried berries (and other fruits) less commonly produced: 1 zante currants; 2 black mulberry; 3 white mulberry; 4 physali; 5 *aronia* (chokeberries); 6 sea-buckthorn; 7 raspberry; 8 kumquats; 9 white raisins (dried in the shade), 10 blueberries; 11 *goji*; 12 cherries; 13 cranberries; 14 sour cherries; and 15 barberries.

Danish desserts.[6] Many of the simple berry dishes prepared by modern Scandinavians were likely relished by Vikings; Norwegian *multekrem* (cloudberries whipped with cream) and Swedish *lingongrädde* (lingonberry cream) would certainly have been as loved by ancient Norsefolk as they are by modern ones. When not turning bilberries into pies, Finns still eat them simply with milk, as they have for centuries.

In the wide chasm between the world's berry pies and puddings, there are hundreds of ways to eat berries and at every time of day. Some of the best-known berry dishes are also some of the oldest, but even recent additions have become iconic.

Italians have bread and jam for breakfast, and Scottish kids eat jam sandwiches (also known as pieces and jam, or

Rødgrød med flode, or red groats with vanilla sauce, is a Scandinavian pudding made with red summer berries.

jeely pieces) for lunch. The English apply jam and clotted cream to scones during afternoon tea, while Russians stir jam directly into their tea. Swedes eat meatballs with lingonberry jam for dinner, and then they have some cloudberry jam with *ostkaka* – their version of cheesecake – for dessert. Jam has been stirred into cocktails since the 1850s. With its appearance at every meal and in-between repast, berry jam has long bridged all the gaps between breakfast and a nightcap.

In Serbian homes, guests are traditionally issued a spoonful of *slatko* and a glass of water as a gesture of hospitality when they are seated. This fruit preserve is most typically made with strawberries, but other fruits (such as quince) are also common. Chokeberries (*Aronia* spp.) are used for making jam in the Balkans. When not eaten directly from a host's spoon, *slatko* is eaten on ice cream or in pancakes.

In Slavic and Baltic states, including Poland and Finland, a gelled berry juice dish called *kissel*, which dates back to the tenth century, is typically made with the sweetened juice of blackberries, blackcurrants or bilberries, thickened with either corn starch or potato starch. The *Gelbe* (gold) version is made with yellow gooseberries or other yellow fruits.

When she wasn't discovering radioactive elements and winning Nobel Prizes, physicist and chemist Marie Curie evidently perfected her gooseberry jelly recipe in 1898 – one month after discovering polonium. Seasonal jam-making expenses were frequently listed in her home account books. Fortunately, fruits that are naturally high in pectin, as gooseberries are, don't require an advanced chemistry degree to be preserved; it just takes the right balance of sugar and acidity and the application of heat.

Blackberries, cranberries and currants are all high in pectin, but eventually American settlers learned to boil pectin out of apples to get berry jellies besides currant to set. Before this trick came along, Hannah Glasse's *The Art of Cookery* (1747) included a recipe for currant jelly, followed by one for 'raspberry giam', made by adding mashed and stewed raspberries

Kissel (a thickened fruit juice) being made in Kiev, from the 15th-century *Radziwiłł Chronicle*.

to her currant jelly, using the latter to set the former. Interestingly, later editions of her book (namely, the 1765 edition) call for a brandy-soaked paper to be applied to tops of the gallipots (glazed ceramic jars), which would have effectively served as a primitive sterile lid. It would be several decades before Parisian confectioner Nicolas-François Appert hermetically sealed glass jars of jam and jelly in a boiling water bath.

Two types of fruit preserve were mentioned in Ottoman palace records: there were thick, pulpy jams called *rub* and whole sweet pickles called *murabbâ* that somewhat resemble Eastern European *varenye*. Some of these, produced specifically for the court elites, were made with barberries, Indian gooseberries and mulberries. Indian gooseberry (amla) has been used in chutneys since time immemorial, and the Indian cooks' skill at transforming sour fruits into succulent chutneys certainly went far in ingratiating them to jam-loving British colonialists.

The British would also develop a taste for Indian jelly made from tipparee, or cape gooseberry (also known as ground cherry or goldenberry), as evidenced by the recipe in the 1907 edition of *Mrs Beeton's Book of Household Management*. (Rasbhari chutney is still made from cape gooseberries today.) This jam was also prepared by the Amish and Mennonites of Pennsylvania, who had immigrated from Germany in the eighteenth century, as mentioned in Edith Thomas's *Mary at the Farm and Book of Recipes Compiled During Her Visit Among the 'Pennsylvania Germans'* (1915). The diminutive tomatillo relative is packed with pectin, making a very easy jam. Goldenberry jam is still eaten in Peru and throughout Africa.

The peanut butter and jelly sandwich is really not that different from any other presentation of sweet preserves with a savoury protein. Lingonberry jam with black pudding or a leg of reindeer; barberries and apples with roast Michaelmas

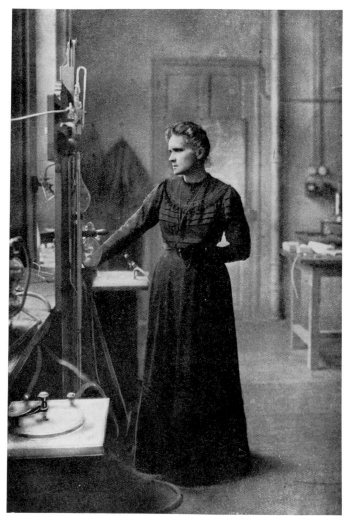

Nobel Prize-winning chemist and physicist Marie Curie enjoyed making
gooseberry jam in her spare time, and kept meticulous notes on her recipes
and process.

Blackberry jam advertisement from a 1948 issue of *Ladies' Home Journal*.

goose: savoury pairings with jam are as old as sweet ones. Gervais Markham also gives a recipe for young or 'green' gosling with gooseberry sauce in his book *The English Huswife* (1615). Resembling an elongated Hot Pocket, the Bedfordshire clanger has taken care of meat and pudding in one convenient pastry-wrapped package since at least the nineteenth century, with meat and potatoes at one end and jam at the other.

Cranberry Sauce

Cranberry sauce is de rigueur on the American Thanksgiving table, but there is no evidence that it was present during the very first Thanksgiving feast between the Pilgrims and the Wampanoag people in 1621. Because its origin is the red-currant sauce of England, recipes adapted to use readily available cranberries appear in the first American cookbook. Amelia Simmons's *American Cookery* (1798) calls for a presentation familiar to anyone who has had Thanksgiving dinner: stuff the turkey with bread dressing flavoured with thyme and marjoram, and then 'serve up with boiled onions and cramberry-sauce' and a side of buttery mashed potatoes and gravy. She doesn't give a recipe for the 'cramberry-sauce', though, so it might be presumed that the condiment was already part of the cook's repertoire.

Cranberry sauce is almost exclusively served at Thanksgiving in the u.s. and Canada, or at Christmas in Canada and the uk, and in these cases, it's mostly the tinned or jarred version. Thanks to IKEA, lingonberry jam is now widely available to those wanting the Scandinavian version for roast turkey (or venison, potato dumplings or meatballs). Redcurrant jelly can similarly be enjoyed any time, particularly with lamb cooked as a Sunday roast.

Bar-le-Duc Jelly

Queen Mary Stuart of France called Bar-le-Duc jelly 'a ray of sunshine in a jar' right around the time that the redcurrant was first domesticated in Europe in the sixteenth century, which means that for two centuries, the jelly was made entirely from wild currants growing around Bar-le-Duc in Lorraine, France. This conserve, a preserve made with whole fruits instead of mashed, was made from red or white currants – only the *versaillaise* or the *roudom* varieties – from which the seeds had been painstakingly removed with a goose-feather quill, all while keeping the berries intact. The process takes a mountain of patience and surgeon-like focus. Naturally, it was made by monks.

Because of the labour involved (not to mention the price of sugar and crystal jars for bottling), Bar-le-Duc jelly was a prohibitively expensive gift passed around among the social elite for centuries, but after the Second World War sales waned. By the 1970s there was only one person left making

A Swedish meal of blood pudding and lingonberry preserves with potatoes and cucumber salad.

White currants like these are used to make one variety of the exquisite Bar-le-Duc jelly. The seeds are removed with a feather quill.

it, and at 91 years old, he was ready to retire. That man, M. Amiable, reluctantly trained his replacement and then sold the business to him. The currants are still seeded excruciatingly by hand, but now instead of monks, it's a group of ten women called *épépineuses* who undertake this task; the fruit are then preserved whole in a thick sugar syrup and poured into small faceted jars. And the jelly is still quite expensive: an 85-g (3-oz) jar will set one back around £20.

Famous Pies and Tarts

Yet another use for redcurrant jam is in the national pride of Austria: the Linzertorte. Originating in the mid-seventeenth century, this thick, crumbly hazelnut pastry is filled with redcurrant or raspberry jam and topped with an intricate pastry lattice. A smaller biscuit version called Linzer sablés (or Linzer cookies in the u.s.) is popular at Christmas, comprising two thin hazelnut shortbread cookies sandwiched with raspberry or currant jam, with the top biscuit having a pretty, decorative pane cut out to reveal the red jam interior.

Although the Linzertorte claims to be the oldest cake in the world, it's really more like a pie, and there are definitely older pies. There are older jam tarts, for that matter, and the jam tart is an even closer approximation to a Linzertorte. Although the earliest ones were more meat-based, crostata date back to the medieval era, with a savoury recipe appearing in Maestro Martino's *Libro de arte coquinaria* (Art of Cooking, 1465) and a sweet version coming before the end of the fifteenth century. Nowadays sweet crostata are typically made of short pastry slathered in jam (raspberry is a common flavour), with a pastry lattice (or sometimes torn pastry) topping. In Argentina, Uruguay, Paraguay and Greece, a similar tart called *pastafrola* is sometimes made with strawberry jam and served as an afternoon dessert. A free-form version of this pie, the galette, is a rustic French alternative to crostata that can use berries or jam (or other fruits).

Classic jam tarts have long offered a way to enjoy the flavour of berries any time of year. Jam pairs well with cheese, too. In Iceland, they serve cheese pizza with berry jam, somewhat akin to a savoury berry-cheese Danish, and cheesecakes are universally improved by berry compotes. Mrs Beeton gives several recipes for berry jam tarts and crème tartlets in the 1861 edition of her *Book of Household Management*. Some, such as the Manchester tart, take the jam pie and add a thick layer of custard and coconut.

And then there's the Bakewell pudding, originally just egg custard and almond flavouring baked over a thick layer of jam. When Eliza Acton wrote about the Bakewell pudding in 1845, she noted that it was famous even outside Bakewell, Derbyshire. By the time Isabella Beeton wrote about the dish less than two decades later, the Bakewell pudding had evolved into a tart, with a pastry shell, a much thinner layer of strawberry jam and another pastry shell encasing it (a second recipe given calls for bread crumbs in lieu of pastry) The Bakewell tart is now a flaky shortcrust shell filled with a thin layer of berry jam and an almond frangipane, and the top may be gilded with icing or slivered almonds.

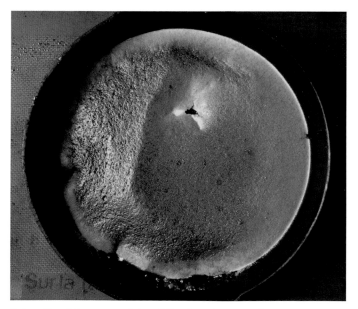

Bakewell pudding prepared from Eliza Acton's 1845 recipe.

Adding a layer of convenience to a jam tart, turnovers are hand-held, enclosing the jam in pastry to prevent sticky messes; going a step further, Pop Tarts are sold in boxes of individually wrapped pastries for cooking right in the toaster. Two of the original Pop Tarts flavours introduced in 1964 were strawberry and blueberry, and Pillsbury Toaster Strudels have always included berry flavours as well. Other hand-sized fruit pies can resemble fat dessert pierogi, such as Hostess fruit pies; they can be deep-fried, such as Hubig's pies in New Orleans (though Scotland can almost certainly be thanked for this invention).

There are several iterations of the personal-sized fruit pie sold at McDonald's worldwide; in the u.s., strawberry-cream pies are available in most locations; in Hong Kong, apple pies

Saskatoon berry pie and saskatoon berry ice cream at a diner in Alberta, Canada.

are served à la mode in a bowl full of strawberry compote; in Germany, diners may treat themselves to a blueberry cheesecake *Tasche* ('bag'). Burger King also sell 'wild berry' flavoured fruit pies.

While any kind of berry can go into a pie or tart shell, there are some particularly famous pies around the world. There's the *blåbärspaj* (bilberry pie) of Sweden, with just a touch of lemon zest and cinnamon, served with *vaniljsås* (vanilla sauce). There are mixed summer-berry pies such as bumbleberry or jumbleberry pie; there's razzleberry (raspberry-blackberry) pie; and there's the late-spring favourite, strawberry-rhubarb pie (also available in the form of a crumble). Rhubarb has been grown for about four hundred years in the UK, whence Americans in New England and Appalachia (where the pie is regionally significant) originally brought it. Deep-dish versions of the pie appeared on American menus in the 1910s.

In the late nineteenth and early twentieth centuries the Frisbie Pie Company in Bridgeport, Connecticut, sold its pies in tin pie plates. At some undocumented point, people began to realize that flying the tins back and forth through the air was pretty fun. In 1939 Middlebury College laid claim to the invention of the game, which was then contested by other eastern colleges. Regardless, the game was spreading like a hot rumour, and in the 1940s, a plastic version of the disc was invented and marketed as a toy flying saucer nationwide. Wham-O purchased this design in 1957 and named it 'Frisbee' after the popular game, not realizing that said game of 'Frisbie' had been named after the pie company whose plates served as the original prototype. Accounting for the toy's spread has been a lot more straightforward since the Second World War, but, said a Wham-O spokesperson, 'as to the documentation on who cast the first one without a blueberry pie in it, that's a bit of a challenge.'[7]

Just as Midwestern food writers recall the pies of their German grandmothers, Canadians have passed along generations of the tradition of picking saskatoon berries to make the pies that their elder women made. Saskatoon berry pie is part of the Canadian culinary heritage, but certainly extended south; one early twentieth-century recipe for 'service-berry pie' comes from a Kentucky housewife, calling for a pint of gooseberries to balance the sweetness of half a gallon of serviceberries.

Cobblers, Buckles, Crisps, Crumbles, Slumps and Grunts

On the theme of 'put berries and something doughy in a dish; cook' there are dozens of variations. Early American settlers brought pudding recipes from England, and these evolved into new dishes. The grunt or slump, for instance, is everything that goes into a steamed pudding (berries with thick batter or dough), but the dough goes on top and it's all cooked on the stove without steaming – the berries cook the batter from below as they stew. The difference in names is geographical; Cape Codders call it a grunt, and the rest of New England calls it a slump. However, if the dish is baked in an oven rather than cooked on the stovetop, it's a cobbler, unless the berries are on top of the dough, in which case it's now a buckle. A cobbler resembles a cobblestone street when it's baked (or it's 'cobbled' together – the jury's still out on that), whereas berries on top cause the dish to buckle inward. The English call a crisp a crumble, but the real difference between the two appears to be whether or not oats are added to the topping.

Blueberry crisp with an oat-almond topping.

Puddings and Dumplings

Blancmanges – those ornate, moulded, jelled milk and starch puddings that have come nearly to define the Victorian dessert tray (though they were invented centuries earlier) – have been berry-flavoured with more regularity over the past century. In rare cases, the name has been adjusted to account for this, as in the case of the *rouge mange*, coloured and flavoured with cranberry juice, which appeared in an 1819 issue of *The Farmer's Magazine*. 'I may now add, that the juices of many other fruits will serve as a substitute for that of the cranberry, when it cannot be procured,' noted the correspondent, who found that the potato starch used in Russian blancmange made a perfectly serviceable thickener.[8] 'I have tried those of the raspberry, currant, orange, &c. and found them to answer very well, although by no means equal to those of the former,' he asserted.[9]

Summer pudding with a variety of berries.

Bready, steamed and boiled puddings have also long been improved by adding berries, and the summer pudding is an exemplary testament to that. Served with globs of creamy custard, spotted dick is a pudding of particular cultural significance for the British, but is a relatively recent addition considering that puddings have been in the national culinary lexicon for centuries. The giggle-inducing name comes from the currants or raisins, which are the spots; the 'dick' likely comes from the German word *dick*, meaning thick, heavy or swollen, which, let's face it, is not much better.

Locker room humour aside, the first recipe for spotted dick appeared in Alexis Sawyer's 1849 *The Modern Housewife or Menagerie* and called for raisins, but modern recipes nearly universally call for dried currants. Mrs Isabella Beeton doesn't share (by name, anyway) a recipe for spotted dick in her *Book of Household Management* of 1861 but does include numerous recipes for other currant puddings, and her boiled currant pudding is a dead ringer. Today, tinned, microwavable spotted dick is available under the Heinz or Simpson's brands, but many home cooks find that nothing beats a fresh, hot spotted dick.

The jam roly-poly is another old-fashioned pud still somewhat in British rotation. This is a suet pudding (a dough made of flour and suet), rolled flat and smeared with jam before being rolled back up like a Swiss roll. The whole affair is steamed in cloth as a cylinder; the name 'dead man's leg' (or sometimes, 'dead man's arm') comes from the long-abandoned practice of using an old trouser leg or shirt sleeve to hold the pudding for steaming. As one of the classic school dinner desserts, it's a collective childhood memory of British Baby Boomers.

Ethnic Germans living in Russia between the 1760s and the turn of the twentieth century particularly loved berry dumplings. Strawberry dumplings called *Erdbeerklösse* (or *Ebenglace* in the Volga or Black Sea German dialect) were eaten as an entrée with sausages; these dumplings are stuffed with chopped strawberries, cooked by boiling in water and then tossed in melted butter and cream. A compote of black nightshade berries (*Schwartzbeeren*; also known as wonderberry), too, could be used to fill the ravioli-like *Maultaschen*, or served over plain dumplings with melted butter and cream, similar to *Ebenglace*, in addition to being enjoyed on *Kuchen* (cakes) or in pies.

Berry dumplings were enjoyed by Jewish cooks as well. Recipes for huckleberry dumplings (and loganberry, in an Oregon version) appear in Jewish cookbooks from the 1910s; these are essentially simple, softball-sized puddings resembling matzo balls, simmered in the juices released by stewing berries. One early African American cookbook, Rufus Estes's *Good Things to Eat* (1911), also includes a recipe for raspberry

A Jell-O advertisement depicting happy kewpie doll children, from *c.* 1915. Two of the original seven flavours were berry flavours.

dumplings where the berries are the filling for soft rice balls
boiled in pudding cloths.

Fools, Custards and Trifles

A fool is a soft custard with fruit – very often berries – folded
in. Gooseberry fool has been a welcome sight at the dessert
table since at least the seventeenth century, when the first
recipe was printed, but mentions of 'foole' date back a century prior. The Italian version of a fool, *zabaglione*, is frequently
served with berries on top or on the side, rather than folded in.

The trifle is somewhat like a layered fool with sponge cake
or ladies' fingers in the bottom of a deep, glass dish. A recipe
appears in *The Good Huswifes Jewell* (1585), but other early versions tend to lack the sponge. The modern version of the
dessert is attributed to Hannah Glasse, whose *Art of Cookery
Made Plain and Simple* (1764) instructs the cook to top a layer
of wine-soaked biscuits, cakes and macaroons with custard
and a layer of syllabub (sweetened, whipped cream), topped
with currant jelly and more crumbled biscuits.

An American approximation of the trifle once graced
American grocery aisles, too. Berry-flavoured instant gelatine
desserts had been introduced in the 1890s under the name
Jell-O, but in 1969 Jell-O released Jell-O 1-2-3 – a mix that
magically self-separated into three layers: a gelatine layer, a
mousse-like middle layer and an airy chiffon topping. Sadly,
the magic wasn't enough to keep shoppers interested. Jell-O
1-2-3 was discontinued three decades later.

However, Jell-O salads have not gone the way of 1-2-3.
Fruit 'salads' of berries, marshmallows and God knows what
else, suspended in lurid, gelled rings, have tenaciously sur-
vived since their zenith in the 1960s. They may have waned in

popularity in recent decades, but the churchgoing housewives of the American Midwest are doing their damnedest to keep the tradition alive. Popular amateur cooking websites such as All Recipes and Taste of Home continue to feature hundreds of Jell-O salads in all their poorly lit glory.

Another American amalgamation, the strawberry delight, is what happens when one mixes strawberry Jell-O, ambrosia salad and cheesecake. It consists of a graham cracker crust topped with a mix of whipped topping (usually Cool Whip), cream cheese and strawberries, with mini marshmallows and sometimes canned fruit cocktail mixed in. A layer of straw-berry Jell-O is then poured over the top and allowed to set. It's most often seen at Middle American potlucks and box-wine-soaked baby showers.

Strawberry Shortcake

Proto-shortcakes from the medieval era tended towards using cinnamon and ginger to flavour the strawberries, and used a flat pastry resembling a pie shell (or sometimes broken pie crust). By the 1860s, however, strawberry shortcake recipes had emerged that more closely resemble the modern version, thanks to liberal use of leavening agents. The strawberry shortcake recipe in *The Practical Cook Book* (1864) calls for the shortcakes to be stacked as a layer cake, with macerated berries and cream between the layers.

A similar 1878 recipe printed in the *New York Times* instructs the reader to prepare a soft yeast- and baking-powder-risen dough that, through its use of eggs, butter, milk and sugar, resembles brioche. Like those in *The Practical Cook Book*, the dough for each shortcake is divided and rolled 'quite thin' into two rounds (1.5 cm, or half an inch, was thin enough in the earlier recipe), which are baked stacked and would rise in the oven somewhat like hamburger buns. The pair is pulled apart while still warm from the oven, the fresh strawberries are lightly mashed between the two cakes, and the whole affair is topped with more berries, sugar and cream.

It took only a few years before cooks began making individual strawberry shortcakes using what is essentially a scone dough leavened with a mix of baking soda and cream of tartar (which yields the same result as baking powder) instead of yeast. In *Mrs. Lincoln's Boston Cook Book: What to Do and What Not to Do in Cooking* (1884), the shortcake dough is rolled and cut out in rounds before baking (or cooking on a griddle), and when baked, the rest of the directions yield something very much like a modern strawberry shortcake: 'Mash a pint of strawberries, sweeten to taste, put a large spoonful on each cake; then put another layer of cakes, and whole berries, well sugared. Serve with cream.'[10]

Originating at Eton College, the Eton Mess is a variation on the theme emerging from the same era (the early 1890s), resembling a strawberry shortcake-parfait hybrid with broken meringue instead of the soft biscuit. Posh versions can tread into pavlova territory, with berries and whipped cream sandwiched between two large meringues, or can use macarons instead of crumbled meringues.

One version of strawberry shortcake beloved by girls in the 1980s is not a food at all. Released in 1980, the berry-scented Strawberry Shortcake dolls were so popular that soon the pop culture landscape was inundated with Strawberry Shortcake playsets, accessories, cartoons, books and even a video game for the Atari 2600. Strawberry Shortcake also released several children's records in the 1980s, including a pop album in 1981 called *Strawberry Shortcake Live* wherein she and her fruity friends rap cloyingly about berries à la The

Classic American-style strawberry shortcake with biscuits and whipped cream.

Sugarhill Gang's 'Rappers' Delight', and sing a nightmarish cover of Kool and the Gang's 'Celebration'.

Strawberry Shortcake received a twenty-first-century makeover, slimming her down a few stone, upgrading her yarn ringlets to a sleeker mane, changing out her white bloomers for capri pants, and replacing her aloof cat Custard with a mobile phone. She's still strawberry-scented, though, allowing girls to experience their first whiff of 'proper' femininity if they are to attain that perfect balance of innocence and allure. Strawberry scents are marketed to adult women as well as little girls, in everything from lip gloss and shampoos to massage oils and sexual lubricants.

Though she's gone through many changes, Strawberry still has her gang of fruit-scented friends, including the Twain-inspired Huckleberry Pie, the catty Raspberry Tart and her dippy bestie Blueberry Muffin.

Blueberry Muffins

Americans love blueberries, long a symbol of luxury at the breakfast table. They even love cramming blueberries into foods where they have no business, such as bagels, trotted out sometime in the late 1980s or early 1990s to appeal to the gentile market. 'The low point [in bagel history] was reached with the introduction of the blueberry bagel – sweet, soft, inky-coloured and hard to tell from a stale doughnut,' wrote journalist William Safire for the *New York Times*, in a sentiment echoed by innumerable other critics.[11]

Unlike blueberry buns – the jammy, fruit-filled rolls much loved by generations of Toronto Jews (but unknown elsewhere) – blueberry bagels sit squarely at the North American culinary nadir; they are mediocrity incarnate at best, and at worst, an offensive form of cultural appropriation. Although doughy American bagels are already a pretty far cry from the authentic Eastern European article, the addition of blueberries has been considered especially deplorable.

One place blueberries do belong, however, is in a muffin. Blueberry muffins are the best-selling pastry at 7-Eleven

Blueberry muffins.

stores, and for good reason. Buttery little mini-cakes studded with juicy berries have always paired well with coffee, making them an obvious fit for the breakfast table or on the go.

Although American cookbooks began including scant recipes for cakey baked muffins by about the 1830s, it took about fifty years before 'huckleberry cakes' – the spitting image of modern blueberry muffins – appeared in *Mrs. Lincoln's Boston Cook Book*. Within a decade, the *Boston Cooking-school Cookbook* had a recipe for berry muffins as well, suggesting they stuck to New England for a while before spreading to the rest of the country (which makes sense since the blueberry is native to New England). A few years later, Chicago-based Rufus Estes included a 'berry muffin' recipe with blueberries in *Good Things to Eat*, and it didn't take long for newspapers on the west coast to extol the joys of a blueberry muffin.

Blueberry Pancakes

Scandinavians have long eaten their various pancakes with lingonberry jam – even the pancake called *Blodplättar* ('plate-lets'), made with pig or reindeer blood. Pancakes may date back to ancient Rome, but the idea to add blueberries to the batter is an American one, and oddly, it appears that no one thought of doing so until the end of the nineteenth century. In the story *Eyebright* (1879) by Susan Coolidge, the protagonist visits a country house in coastal Maine, where she's met with a new dining experience:

> Did any of you ever eat blueberry flapjacks? I imagine not, unless you have summered on the coast of Maine. They are a kind of greasy pancake, in which blueberries are stirred till the cakes are about the colour of a bruise.

They are served swimming in melted butter and sugar, and in any other place or air would be certain indigestion, if not sudden death, to any person partaking of them. But, somehow, in that place and that air they are not only harmless but seem quite delicious as well. Eyebright thought so. She ate a great many flapjacks, thought them extremely nice, and slept like a top afterward, with never a bad dream to mar her rest.[12]

It didn't take long for blueberry pancakes to spread from New England to the rest of the country; however, nowadays most places gently fold the berries in rather than beating them to a bruise hue. As with blueberry muffins, the earliest recipes for blueberry pancakes seem to be regional. *Mrs. Lincoln's Boston Cook Book* offers the earliest facsimile with huckleberry griddle cakes.

Confectionery

Berry-flavoured candies and confections are enjoyed by the sweet-toothed worldwide. Even chocolates are paired with berries, as anyone on an unimaginative Valentine's Day date can testify. Chocolate-dipped strawberries seem fairly to exemplify the boorish decadence of the American 1980s, in some coke-addled attempt to harness the fondue craze of the 1960s with the addition of convenience.

But candy-covered fruits are nothing new, nor were they borne of nouveau riche excess. Chinese people have loved candied hawthorn berries for ages. In northern China, childhood memories are made on *bingtanghulu* – whole hawthorn berries as big as crab apples, impaled on a bamboo skewer, coated in a hard candy shell and sprinkled with sesame seeds.

Sold by street vendors, strawberries and blueberries are also commonly turned into *tanghulu* these days. (Chinese people also love hawthorn in other forms, as seen in the slightly sour discs of dried hawthorn pulp known as haw flakes.)

Of course, Chinese people aren't the only ones with a penchant for candied berries. The German candy company Haribo makes a line of realistic-looking berry-flavoured gummies called Raspberries, and centuries earlier, Georgian confectioners were fairly obsessed with gooseberry 'hops'.

The first recipe, 'To preserve Gooseberries in Hops', from *The Compleat Housewife* (1727), called for berries to be impaled on 'fine long thorns'.[13] A later version of the process detailed in *The Housekeeper's Instructor* (1792) was safer but still fairly involved: five or six gooseberries were split into quarters lengthwise, leaving them attached at the stem end. These were stacked together, alternating the berries by ninety degrees so that they resembled a hops cone. They were then strung

Haribo-brand gummy raspberries and blackberries.

Blackcurrant *zefir*s at a Russian market.

through with a needle and thread and knotted to keep them securely attached before being candied in a thick lemon-ginger syrup.

A variety of berry candies have been popular in Russia for centuries. In particular, *zefir*s are marshmallow meringues sometimes encased in chocolate; they are named after the Greek wind deity Zephyr because of the confection's airiness. Invented by Russian confectioners in the fifteenth century, *zefir*s were traditionally made with apple purée and often flavoured with mashed sour berries (lingonberry or rowan). The confection is related to the traditional Russian *pastila*, a cross between a marshmallow and Turkish delight, but it wasn't until French confectioners in the nineteenth century began adding meringue to the same formula that modern *zefir*s were born. They are so integral to the culinary heritage of Kolomna, Russia, that there's a museum dedicated to the confection there.

Soup, Porridge and Drinks

Europeans with a penchant for snow sports have taken to chugging warm berry purée, as in the case of the Swedish bilberry soup *blåbärssoppa* (the Finnish version is *mustikkakeitto*). Similar to an un-gelled *Kissel*, it can be served hot or cold, but since it's commonly drunk from a mug after skiing, it's best served warm. Kept warm in an insulated flask, *blåbärssoppa* is the unofficial beverage of Vasa Loppet, the Swedish ski marathon. Other berry soups are enjoyed across Eastern Europe as well, with or without skis.

Chilled berry sherbets in Ottoman cuisine lie somewhere between a drink and a soup; they can be drunk from a glass or slurped from a spoon. German royal confectioner Friedrich Unger noted in the 1830s a dozen or so flavours of sherbet made by an Istanbul confectioner, which included raspberry and barberry. Sherbet would eventually evolve into the frozen dessert sorbet, but *sharbat* (from the Arabic *shariba*, meaning 'to drink', as is 'syrup') is still a sweet beverage enjoyed throughout the Middle East and northern Africa, and led to the sweet vinegar-based berry syrups of seventeenth-century England called shrubs.

Berry syrups would go on to become the basis of numerous drinks, including the spiced berry squash enjoyed everywhere but the Americas, sometimes with raspberry vinegar mixed in. The drink mix Kool-Aid was originally made from syrups until its inventor figured out a way to save shipping costs by dehydrating it to a powder in the 1920s. Two of the original six flavours – raspberry and strawberry – are still sold. The phrase 'drink the Kool-Aid' is colloquially used to convey the lemming-like behaviour exhibited by the 907 people who were brainwashed into committing mass suicide in what has been dubbed the Jonestown Massacre of

1978. However, it was a cheaper knock-off of Kool-Aid called Flavor Aid that was used to administer the cocktail of cyanide and sedatives, and it wasn't a berry flavour. It was grape.[14]

Juices and Smoothies

Counter to fruit-flavoured suicide cocktails, berry smoothies have been promoted as a key to good health since the 1960s. If the bobby-socks-wearing 1950s are burgers and milkshakes, the groovy 1960s are exemplified by granola and smoothies. The first smoothies were sold by a lactose-intolerant soda jerk named Steve Kuhnau, who had begun experimenting with dairy-free alternatives to milkshakes. He opened a health food store in Louisiana in 1973, selling his new fruit-, vitamin- and protein-packed creations, which he called 'smoothies'. They were so popular that by 1989 he had begun the franchise Smoothie King, which has more than 550 locations in the u.s. and spurred an entire juicing movement. Now there are tens of thousands of places to drink smoothies worldwide. Even McDonald's sells berry smoothies.

Berry teas and other drinks have long histories in Europe. Usually made from cranberries and lingonberries, *mors* is one that's been part of the Russian culinary lexicon for centuries. The *Domostroy*, a sixteenth-century encyclopaedia of household rules, covered everything from advice on how to punish an unruly son to instructions for making a good *mors*. Today, shop-bought cranberry juice cocktail, first created by the cranberry-growing cooperative Ocean Spray (who also invented the juice box and the grocery store juice aisle), comes somewhat close.

Another berry drink called *kompot* can be made with a variety of berries, and was invented as a way to preserve

Cranberry juice is a common cocktail mixer, as seen in this holiday variation on a Moscow mule.

whole fruits. *Kompot* is drunk throughout Southern, Central and Eastern Europe, and is still popular in Central Asia, but with the introduction of bottled juice and sodas to these parts of the world in the 1980s, its popularity has waned somewhat.

Berry juices were a very popular alternative to alcoholic drinks in pre-Prohibition America, and have maintained an ardent following. During Prohibition, some breweries switched to full-time production of sodas to stay afloat; Henry Weinhard's (1856–1999) made several brands of soda during Prohibition (including loganberry and strawberry), marketing them as 'safest for children'.[15] Berry-flavoured sodas have been a mainstay for more than a century; Crush has several berry flavours (including blue raspberry), as does Fanta. There are dozens more worldwide, such as Kracherl in Austria, Orangine and Tropical in Ecuador, and Márka in Hungary.

Berry Beers, Ales and Ciders

Naturally, some people prefer their fizzy berry drinks with a little alcohol, and while it's easy to roll one's eyes at the latest organic, gluten-free, açaí berry 'health' beer, berry beers actually date back centuries. Purportedly of Welsh Druid origin, one old ale called *ebulum* appears in scores of old British brewing books and even travelled to America, appearing in

A selection of Slovakian berry-flavoured teas.

recipe books well into the nineteenth century. It was flavoured with the berries of danewort, also known as dwarf elder. It's since been revived by Scottish brewery the Williams Brothers Brewing Co., who also make seaweed and pine ales based on historic recipes.

Before Germans began using hops in beer-brewing in the twelfth century, the rowan berries called chequers (or wild service) were used to flavour an ale-like drink called chequer ale. Chequer ale-houses may have been so-called because of the chequer ale being served, or the name could be related to the fact that the chequerboard is an ancient symbol of a pub. However, the pub name had originally been brought by the Romans, who used the chequerboard as a symbol that an ale-house also conveniently provided banking services under the same roof; the use of the word 'cheque' for a note of monetary value is derived from the old Norman habit of counting money on a chequered tablecloth. British naturalist Patrick Roper notes on his blog Rowans, Whitebeams and Service Trees that pubs with 'chequer' in the name are typically sited around Kent, Sussex and Surrey, and this is evidenced by early nineteenth-century surveys of those areas.[16]

A French brewers' guide published in 1828 offers instructions on brewing *Bière framboisée dite bière des dames*, or roughly, 'Raspberry Beer, Known as Ladies' Beer'.[17] The strawberry beer Früli is made at the three-hundred-year-old Huyghe brewery near Ghent, Belgium, and it's the Belgians who have maintained mastery of the art of berry beers. A similar beer called lambic is a sour and cidery Belgian beer fermented with wild yeasts and the bacteria of the Zenne valley (where Brussels is located). Lambics are the best known of the Belgian fruit beers, flavoured with berries such as raspberry, blackcurrant and strawberry, or, less commonly, cloudberry. One well-known brand, Lindemans, has been producing lambic since 1822, but didn't deviate away from *kriek* (cherry) until introducing the *framboise* (raspberry) flavour in 1980, and then added *cassis* (blackcurrant) six years later.

Ciders, too, are improved by berries. The dryness of a cranberry is a natural good fit for an austere apple cider, and Belgian cider maker Ruwet (in operation since 1898) makes an elderberry cider. Raspberry, blackberry and currant find their way into ciders worldwide, and rowans have long been used to bolster the flavour of German apple wines.

Berry Wines

People have been making wine with (non-grape) berries for just as long as they have been using grapes. Around 7000–5600 BC, before ordinary wine was invented, the Chinese were purportedly making grape-hawthorn berry wine. *Apicius* recommends keeping mulberries in wine, and a recipe for berry mead appears in *Domostroy*, too, calling for 'berries of any type'.[18] *Bokbunjaju* made in Korea from black raspberries is traditionally sold near the entrance to Bukhansan National Park in the autumn, and is believed to increase male fertility. Mulberry and elderberry wines were much loved throughout antiquity and beyond. In the mid-eighteenth century Hannah Glasse offered recipes for various country wines: elderberry (including one that she says resembles frontignac or moscato), blackberry, gooseberry and currant, each of which are also mentioned in Charles Carter's *The Compleat City and Country Cook; or, Accomplish'd House-wife* (1732). *The Distiller's Guide* (1818) provides instruction on 'The Art of Making British Wines' from the berries 'of the native growth of Great Britain', including the above-mentioned, in addition to strawberries, raspberries and dewberries.[19] By the 1920s American kosher foods company Manischewitz had begun to make Passover wines, which eventually included loganberry, elderberry and blackberry wines.

Chokeberries are also used for making wine in Lithuania, but in the Balkans they are just as frequently added to tea. A variety of other teas can be made with dried berries, such as Twinings's wild berry tea flavoured with (tame) blackcurrants, blueberries, raspberries and strawberries.

Flavoured Spirits

The very first spirits were flavoured with berries (with juniper; although that's technically a cone). Theologian John Knox reported in the 1780s that a dram of whisky, gin, rum or brandy, 'plain or infused with berries that grow among the heath', was the opening act in a healthy Highland breakfast, and berry-flavoured spirits have not gone out of style since.

Various berries have found their way into vodka, rum and tequila – where they perhaps don't belong, despite what sorority girls think. Brandy, however, is a perfectly reasonable place for berry flavours to appear. The raspberry makes a lovely addition to schnapps, as seen in the *Himbeergeist* of Germany and Alsace. Instructions for making raspberry brandy appear in distillers' guides dating back to the 1730s, though 'Raspberry-brandy is in less demand in the country than Cherry-brandy is,' according to *A Compleat Body of Distilling*.[20] This book also offers instructions for making an elderberry-infused spirit. Another guide from 1818 offers many of the same recipes, but includes some simpler alternatives, such as brandy mixed with raspberry juice, which is 'a fine dram'.

Crimean Tatars of Central Asia purportedly distilled a brown liquor they called *arraki* from sloes and wild berries, according to several early nineteenth-century sources. Today Indonesian *arrack* and Middle Eastern *arak* are two very different liquors completely lacking berry infusion. Considering that the rest of Tatar cuisine reflects its Turkic origin, it seems likely that the name *arraki* came from the Middle Eastern *arak*; the word *aragh* is used colloquially to mean vodka by Iranians, Armenians and people living in the Caucasus.

Another nearby and closely named spirit called *raka* was improved by the addition of berries. Before Siberia was Russian, people in Kamchatka distilled liquor from a plant the natives called *slatkaia trava*, meaning 'sweet grass', which botanists referred to as 'spondilium foliole pinnatifide'. This probably refers to the plant *Heracleum sphondylium*, or common hogweed; although the plant is not a grass at all, early descriptions of the 'sweet grass' match that of hogweed completely.

Most telling is this reference to a certain property of the 'sweet grass': 'the juice is so inflammatory that great care is taken in eating them that they shall not touch the lips, for if they should, an immediate blister would be the consequence.' As any hiker who's experienced a brush with this giant angelica relative can attest, a severe case of painful photodermatitis is a common result.[21] The *raka* distilled from this sweet plant was flavoured with wild-gathered *gimolost* or blue honeysuckle (aka haskap). French diplomat Barthélemy de Lesseps, who had travelled Kamchatka in the 1780s, said that 'those who drink of it are sure to be extremely agitated during the night, and to experience on the next day melancholy and disturbed sensations. But, notwithstanding those disadvantages, it is drunk by the inhabitants with extraordinary avidity.'[22]

Cordials and Liqueurs

Spirits infused with fruit are generally known as ratafias, and have been around since at least the late 1600s. They were originally made from stone fruits, but for the past two centuries have also been made in an array of berry flavours such as currant, raspberry, mulberry and gooseberry, each touched with a hint of lemon peel, cinnamon and clove. The name ratafia (and later, 'ratify') comes from the Italian *rata fiat*, or to seal a deal with a toast.

One famous ratafia is *ratafia de cassis*, better known today as crème de cassis. The liqueur appears as a recommended aperitif in a French maternity guidebook in 1777, whose title translates to *The Manual of the Pregnant Women, Those in Childbirth and Mothers Who Want to Feed* (not, sadly, *What to Drink When You're Expecting*). This liqueur ends up in a number of other more expected places such as French kir cocktails, the nicest of which is the kir royale, made by topping crème de cassis with champagne; it's also used to make 'cider and black' by topping it with a float of cider.

Other berry liqueurs have graced drinks cabinets around the world, and several recipes for berry-forward liqueurs and 'marasquins' (maraschinos) appear in Jerry Thomas's tome of mixology, *How to Mix Drinks; or, the Bon Vivant's Companion* (1862). There's raspberry-flavoured Chambord, inspired by the raspberry liqueurs enjoyed by the Louis XIV in the Loire Valley in the seventeenth century but only in production since 1982. Laplanders make a variety of liqueurs and spirits from Arctic brambleberries, whortleberries and cloudberries, keeping them warm on frigid nights, including the sweet Finnish cloudberry liqueur *lakka likööri*. Germans have *Echte Kroatzbeere* blackberry liqueur, and Italians have *fragoli* flavoured with strawberries.

Cocktails

Though they can be drunk with soda water, sweet, berry-forward vinegar syrups called shrubs (not to be confused with the citrus liqueur) can also be cocktail mixers often used in punches. As with so many inventions, these began as a

Kir royale cocktail made with blackcurrant liqueur.

Berry shrub cocktail with lemon garnish.

way to preserve berries, brought to colonial America in the seventeenth century. They have experienced a recent revival with the current trend towards old-timey cocktails.

Since berries are best during the summer, most would agree that cold applications are better suited to berry beverages. But for those who want cold berry beverages all year round, jams can fit the bill in the off-season. Berry syrups appear in dozens of Victorian cocktail recipes, and domesticity manuals, pharmaceutical guides and gentlemen's table guides of the era sometimes called for berries muddled with sugar for drinks. Jam could be stirred into cocktails when fresh fruit wasn't available. Smash cocktails, as these drinks are known, appear on cocktail menus as early as the 1850s.

Besides being a baked dessert, cobblers are the name for another family of cocktails arising from the nineteenth century's burgeoning love of cocktail culture. Defined by a base of sherry or port, citrus and sugar, shaken and served over crushed or 'cobbled' ice, cobblers often include berries. 'The "cobbler" does not require much skill in compounding,' wrote Jerry Thomas in his *Bon-Vivant's Companion*, 'but to make it acceptable to the eye, as well as the palate, it is necessary to display some taste in ornamenting the glass after the beverage is made.'[23] When made to 'suit an epicure' according to the book's illustration and instructions, it is most necessary to feature the berry.[24]

A berry cocktail is a nice way to end one's evening, but history shows us that berries can be put to use in crafting more permanent nightcaps as well.

5
Poison and Panacea

Berries are a 'superfood', promising to cure cancer and lengthen life. They're also the leading cause of accidental poisonings outside of household products. Humans have always been drawn to berries to cure what ails them, but sometimes it's the berries that cause the problems. Many medicinal plants have dangerous relatives, and some genera run a Jekyll and Hyde game on the unsuspecting. Making matters worse, some plants have safe parts *and* poisonous parts, such as the potato, whose berry contains toxic levels of solanine. The 'berries' or arils of the yew tree, nectar-sweet and quite edible, encase a deadly seed, and the tree's bark is so poisonous it can kill cancer cells.

Poison

Back in ye olden times in Sheffield, a 'poison berry' was slang for an ill-tempered woman who spoke ill of her neighbours, her gossip tainting those who bent an ear. Most poison berries don't just spoil civility, however. Berries evolved toxic glucosides and alkaloids to deter ingestion by any animals that won't pass their seeds unscathed: namely, mammals. This is why one should never trust birds to guide one towards safe

The arils of the yew are the only nontoxic part of the plant.

berries – birds eat scads of toxic berries, deposit the seeds all over Creation and live to do it another day. To wit, pokeberries are relished by birds, but a handful will kill a human child.

The plant kingdom is rife with deadly plants, and has provided poisoners with plenty of material for thousands of years. But it's not just the poisoner's deadly nightshades and belladonnas with which one must contend; it's the friendly-looking berries that are most troublesome, particularly in the hands of children. English ivy and Virginia creeper look pastoral, and their juicy purple berries may tempt the unwary. Mistletoe berries look like glossy, white gooseberries; in tandem with the equally toxic berries of festive holly, they could deck the halls . . . with tragedy. Fortunately, these are all so bitter that it's unlikely they will accidentally be eaten in large enough quantities to do much harm. (Then again, toddlers will eat raccoon faeces if left to their own devices.)

Plant-based poisons have long been a readily available way to off one's enemies. Macbeth supposedly used dwale (nightshade) to poison an army of Danes invading Scotland before

Deadly
nightshade
berries.

he became king in 1040, and a millennium earlier, the same
was used to staunch Mark Antony's troops.

Better Call Locusta of Gaul

What was an ancient Roman emperor's wife to do when she
needed to be rid of a drooling, bloodthirsty husband with a
drinking problem? Call her poisoner, that's what. And Locusta
of Gaul was there to oblige.

In the first century AD Nero's mother, Agrippina the
Younger, purportedly hired history's first professional poi-
soner (the first on record, at least) to kill her husband/uncle,
Roman emperor Claudius. After Claudius was murdered,
Locusta was prosecuted for the crime. With his stepfather/

Festive-looking holly berries are poisonous if eaten.

grand-uncle Claudius out of the way, Emperor Nero (who was married to Claudius' daughter, his stepsister/cousin) saved Locusta from execution and kept her on retainer as his own personal assassin. He had her poison his brother Britannicus to eliminate his competition for the throne (after a few stumbles getting the dose right).

Three centuries later, Rome was again besieged by poisoning when as many as 366 women – dubbed the 'matron poisoners' – were accused of compounding fatal potions from various nightshade-family berries and other ingredients.[1]

Poisoner's Handbook

At the turn of the nineteenth century, the world's first toxicologist, Mathieu Orfila, ranked belladonna (a potent nightshade) as an acrid-narcotic for its properties of inducing hallucinations, but as history has shown, the berries were also quite handy at quickly ridding women of their husbands. Besides being used to poison Claudius' mushroom dinner, belladonna was thought to have been used to enhance the arsenic and lead in the Aqua Tofana used to kill six hundred men in seventeenth-century Italy. The poison had been distributed by Giulia Tofana to hundreds of women stuck in bad marriages, particularly the poorer classes who had few (if any) other options for escaping their abusers. 'There was not a lady in Naples who had not some of it lying on her toilet among her perfumes, in a phial known only to herself,' wrote one eighteenth-century commentator.[2] A similar concoction was purportedly used by Adolf Hitler for his suicide, wherein he overdosed on a pill made of belladonna and strychnine, prescribed by his doctor for stomach cramps.

Belladonna berries are seldom the cause of accidental poisoning. Although the glossy black berries look tempting, 'they have a mawkish taste,' warned *A Treatise on Poisons* (1845).[3] The plant's primary alkaloid, atropine, first causes dryness of the throat. Next, the pupils of the eyes dilate, which is why many Italian women took it intentionally – dilated pupils were once considered attractive and this is the basis of the plant's name, *belladonna*, which means 'beautiful lady'. Next comes delirium of the 'generally extravagant' variety; 'also, most commonly of the pleasing kind, sometimes accompanied with immoderate uncontrollable laughter, sometimes with constant talking, but occasionally with complete loss of voice.'[4] There's also a feeling of being in a state of walking twilight sleep, and convulsions, though rare, may occur. In one case a poisoner administered belladonna with the intent of committing a theft while her victim was in a stupor.

Another poison berry, baneberry (*Actaea spicata*), is also called herb Christopher, after its patron saint. The herb was supposedly effective against plague, which makes sense; if one wanted to end one's suffering, one simply had to eat a few of the poisonous berries. It was long listed in witches' grimoires, possibly owing to its association with other organisms associated with witchcraft. 'It is said that toads allured by the foetid smell of this plant resort to it,' wrote one eighteenth-century botanical manual.[5] Being poisoned with baneberry is decidedly less fun than with belladonna; immediate burning in the mouth followed by stomach cramps and vomiting within half an hour means it's unlikely to be eaten in large enough quantities to have a permanent effect.

Most berries that don't taste nice won't be eaten more than once, unless they have something good to offer.

Panacea

In what is perhaps the world's only musical ode to a conserve, 'Blackcurrant Jam', performed by indie rock band Grizzly Bear, rightfully extolls the jam's superlative quality, adding a helpful little titbit about its use as a salve for wounds. It's widely understood that eating fresh fruit is generally good for the health, but berries' other salubrious qualities have been known for millennia. They make good medicine.

Native Americans used various berries for everything from stimulating fertility to soothing fevers. Sea buckthorn was known by Theophrastus and Dioscorides, and clinical trials over the past decade have identified its therapeutic value in cancer treatment. In *On the Properties of Foodstuffs*, second-century physician Galen mentions blackberries as effective at stopping the bowels, and mulberries as aiding digestion; Linnaeus claimed to have to cured his own gout by eating strawberries; and the chequer berry's medicinal properties are revealed in its name – *torminalis* means 'good for colic'.

Nineteenth-century illustration of *Atropa belladonna*, a nightshade whose berries were commonly used by poisoners of classical antiquity.

Blackberry syrup is an antidiarrheal that has been historically used to treat children with cholera, dysentery and 'summer complaint'. Before the advent of modern medicine at the turn of the twentieth century, most people turned to their cookbooks, not doctors, when they were under the weather. For some reason, housewives preferred a blackberry cordial to a ghastly bloodletting.

In 1800 Hannah Glasse and Maria Wilson found berry wines to be 'good in fevers, afflictions of the lungs, prevent the infection of pestilential airs, beget a good appetite, and help digestion; are excellent in surfeits, and purify the blood'.[6] Modern berry drinks such as the English blackcurrant Ribena

Bottled sea buckthorn juice and jelly at a shop in Germany.

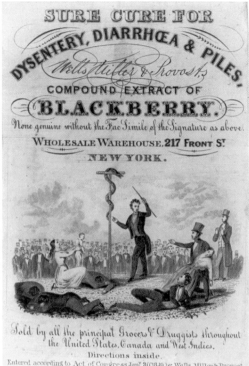

Advertisement for blackberry extract, c. 1849. Blackberry syrups have been used as medicine for centuries.

(named after *Ribes*, or currant) were invented as vitamin C supplements during the Second World War, and today berry drinks are still drunk for their salubrity worldwide.

Elderberry: Cure-all

Tainted elderberry wine may have been used to commit murders in Joseph Kesselring's play *Arsenic and Old Lace*, but elderberry wine has a very long history of being a helpful medicine. 'It is an excellent febrifuge, cleanses the blood of acidity, venom and putrefaction,' wrote Hannah Glasse and Maria Wilson; 'it is good in measles, small-pox, swine-pox, and pestilential diseases; it contributes to rest, and takes away the heat that afflicts the brain.'[7] And if one drank enough of it, perhaps it could afflict the brain with good humours instead.

All parts of the plant have been historically used, as mentioned by Pliny the Elder, but the berries seem to have had the most uses. One book, *Anatomia Sambuci; or, the Anatomie of the Elder* (1677), outlined the 'Plain, Approved, and Specific Remedies for most and chiefest Maladies; Confirmed and cleared by Reason, Experience, and History'.[8] Among the uses mentioned in this monograph, elder was good for soothing an array of uterine disorders, healing ulcers and the bites of mad dogs, and curing epilepsy and the plague, and was an all-around prophylactic against illness. A 'rob' (or sweetened cordial of the berries) was recommended for making various tinctures, or could be taken alone, as was suggested to nursing mothers with sick infants.

Elderberry outranks all other berries in flavonoid content, but even though it's been used for millennia to treat a wide array of ailments, modern studies have not been sufficiently conducted to determine its efficacy as an antioxidant. Nonetheless, elderberry syrups and lozenges are found in numerous natural and alt-health products for treating the symptoms of the common cold and sinus infections. The Swiss company Ricola makes a mixed berry lozenge both flavoured and powered by concentrated extracts of bilberry, raspberry, blackcurrant *and* elderberry – one of the ten 'magic herbs' that have been part of its original formula since the 1940s. But for those who prefer medicines with more of a pharmaceutical kick, berry flavour is also commonly added to over-the-counter and narcotic cough syrups.

Traditional Chinese Medicine

Whereas Chinese desserts are typically egg or rice-based puddings, tarts and custards, they usually eat their berries as medicine. One berry, though, does double duty, serving as a sweet treat as well as medicine. Chinese hawthorn berries, or *tanghulu*, have been candied and sold as a street snack for eight hundred years, dating back to the Song Dynasty (AD 960–1279). A legend tells of an emperor whose favourite concubine fell ill and lost her appetite. A doctor prescribed her ten sugared *tanghulu* daily, and when the concubine healed completely within two weeks, word spread quickly and the vitamin-C-rich berry in a hard candy shell became a popular treat.

Haw flakes are another hawthorn candy that can be used medicinally. The small reddish discs are made of pulverized, sweetened hawthorn and can be the 'spoonful of sugar' to help

Tanghulu (hawthorn berries in a crunchy candy shell) at a street stall in China.

Berry-based health supplements claim to prevent a variety of illnesses.

bitter Traditional Chinese Medicine (TCM) go down, or they can be used alone as a medicine. They have been historically used as a paediatric vermifuge to kill intestinal parasites, but today, the red dyes used to give haw flakes their dark rose colour are banned in several countries.

In China, *wu gu ji tong* – black silkie chicken soup with goji berries – is part of the traditional month-long 'confinement diet' imposed on new mothers right after giving birth. It's thought that the broth, made from a small, black-fleshed breed of chicken, helps bring the mum's milk in, and the goji berries heal her body after childbirth. After their daughters give birth, some wealthier Chinese grandmothers even contract private soup chefs at upwards of £740 ($900) per day as part of an all-inclusive in-home post-partum service to stay and help the new mother recuperate under a watchful eye.

Schisandra, also known as five-flavour berry (or *wu wei zi*), is another ingredient used in TCM that is now being sold as 'the ultimate superberry', promising longevity and vitality.[9] This berry is never candied and sold as a street snack; instead the small red fruit is dried, powdered and added to formulas for everything from fighting inflammation to improving mental health.

Sea buckthorn was used in Chinese, Tibetan and Indian traditional medicine as well, primarily in treating ailments of the skin; similarly, in ancient Greece, the entire plant was fed to horses to give them a glossy coat (the Latin name *Hippophae* means 'shiny horse'). The light-orange berries are well guarded with sharp spines, but once these are removed, the berries can be juiced and bottled, as sold in German and Scandinavian markets. Sea buckthorn shows potential as an antimutagenic, protecting bone marrow from damage during radiation therapy in cancer patients and helping recovery from chemotherapy, but studies on humans are still needed to validate this.

Superfoods

Berries are known as 'superfoods', as they are high in a variety of cancer-fighting phytochemicals called flavonoids and contain the highest concentration of a specific flavonoid – anthocyanin – which primarily functions as a pigment in plants, giving the reddish, bluish and purplish colours of berries. Anthocyanins are also potent antioxidants and show promise in modern treatments of diseases; 'the blacker the berry, the sweeter the juice,' as the saying goes, but also the higher the anthocyanins.

Although many of berries' potentially medical applications are only observed in vitro and not in the human body, as of 2016, newly dubbed 'nutraceuticals' are a £160 ($200) billion industry. Health and beauty products made with chokeberry, wolfberry, hawthorn, bilberry, açaí and another tropical berry, Chilean wild blackberry (*maqui*), are big business in China and Japan. In the West, where complementary alternative medicine like TCM is gaining mainstream acceptance, the sky's the limit for berry supplements.

Those sceptical about allopathic medicine have been drawn to these products, which has made some very rich. Sales of açaí products went through the roof as they burst onto the market, when açaí was promoted on *The Oprah Winfrey Show* by dermatologist Nicholas Perricone as a silver bullet for weight loss and fighting wrinkles (for which açaí has never been demonstrated effective). He sells powdered açaí on his website for $75 for thirty packets.

Although they may relieve some symptoms, supplements and health-food products made of berries have never been scientifically proven effective at controlling or preventing diseases. This hasn't escaped the notice or criticism of some in the scientific community, who accuse the products' manufacturers of charlatanism – and their consumers of delusion. 'By denigrating science, these detractors have enlarged the potential following for magical and pseudoscientific health products,' wrote one outspoken critic for the journal *Academic Medicine*.[10] This scientist identified two basic types of people who buy alternative medicine products: those who are philosophically committed to hippie stuff, and the desperate.

But contrary to so many unproven therapies, science has shown a promising connection between eating berries and killing cancer cells. 'Berries, especially strawberries, raspberries, and blueberries, as well as pomegranates (technically berries) are quite suggestively linked' with longevity and lower rates of cancer and heart disease, wrote anthropologist E. N. Anderson.[11]

Elderberry tinctures and concentrated açaí powders may be no more effective than charms and amulets at prolonging human life, or they may hold secrets which science has yet to quantify. Berries are our food, our drink, our medicine; they get us high, they tell our lore, they underscore our social identities. Though they may be diminutive and endearingly sweet, they should not be underestimated. There is no denying that berries have a magical hold on humans.

Appendix:
Botanical Descriptions

Strawberries (*Fragaria* spp.)

Strawberries produce prostrate, stoloniferous plants that can reproduce sexually (through their seeds) or vegetatively (through their stolons, or runners). Their runners are stems that shoot off and take root, producing clones of their parents. Their leaves are compound, producing three leaflets with jagged margins, and their white flowers are five-petalous. Their 'berries' are typically red (sometimes white or pink) etaerios, consisting of an aggregate of achenes surrounding a fleshy receptacle.

Genetically, strawberries are all over the place. They exhibit a wide variation in polyploidy (the number of pairs of chromosomes), which is a key to their differentiation as distinct species, but more importantly is typically linked to how robust the plants and their fruits are. The diploid species (having two sets of chromosomes) are smaller, with more reduced fruits, whereas the decaploid species (with ten sets of chromosomes) have produced commercial varieties. One decaploid species, *F. cascadensis*, grows wild in the Cascade Mountains of Oregon, and is currently being hybridized with other decaploid cultivars in search of new commercial varieties.

Brambles (*Rubus* spp.)

The brambles, or cane-berries, include many hundreds of wild and cultivated shrubs. Although *Rubus* is an exceedingly diverse genus, blackberries, raspberries and everything in between share some overarching similarities: a few are orange or yellow, but they're mostly red, blue or black etærios of tiny, juicy drupes – fleshy, thin-skinned fruits surrounding a single pip. These are arranged on a tender, white receptacle; in blackberries, this remains part of the berry when picked, but in raspberries, the receptacle stays attached to the stem, leaving a hollow berry.

There are three main types of blackberry, differentiated by their growth habits: erect, semi-erect and trailing. These groups were known previously (at the turn of the twentieth century) as high blackberries, half-highs and dewberries, respectively. With their prostrate, rambling vines, trailing blackberries such as dewberry, loganberry and boysenberry are a tad fussier than other blackberries, preferring milder winters and clear summers, so even though they're available in thornless varieties, some gardeners find their cultivation not worth the trouble. The half-high, semi-erect blackberries are typically thornless and bear flavourful fruit, making them an obvious choice for home gardens. Erect or high blackberries, while painfully armed, are the prolific bearers of the world's largest blackberries – the Kiowa variety produces fruits up to 8 cm (3 in.) long.[1]

Serviceberry (*Amelanchier* spp.)

The botanical treatment of serviceberry has perhaps been simpler than that of *Rubus*, but one botanist lamented in 1912 that 'it is with some hesitation that the writer attempts a treatment of a genus which in the past has been subject to so much difference of opinion as has *Amelanchier*.'[2] To be specific, the botanist in question, Karl McKay Wiegand of the New England Botanical Club and head of the Department of Botany at Cornell University, noted that identification had become somewhat cumbersome owing to the great phenotypic variation displayed by the genus.[3]

Wiegand's assessment of *Amelanchier*'s wide heterogeneity is certainly substantiable, with twenty or so species ranging in habit from small trees to prostrate shrubs. The plants are native to the Northern Hemisphere, but the largest diversity of species is seen in northeastern North America, where Wiegand studied them. The genus would continue to perplex botanists well into the 1990s, until molecular techniques could begin to settle its taxonomy. Wanton hybridization, polyploidy and asexual seed production have all played a role in making species identification a rather tricky business.

Thankfully, some characteristics are nearly universally shared among serviceberries. The leaves are deciduous and smooth, for instance (though some have serrated edges just at the apex); the five-petalled flowers, growing in clusters, are showy and white (though sometimes yellow or pink). The spherical fruits resemble miniature reddish to dark bluish-purple apples, complete with tiny lenticels freckling the skin and flayed-out sepals encircling the crumbly brown stigma at the base like a wee crown.[4]

Rowan (*Sorbus* spp.)

Rowan is a small tree that grows throughout the temperate regions of the Northern Hemisphere, with pinnately compound leaves that somewhat resemble those of an ash tree (*Fraxinus* spp.), lending the rowan its American name, mountain ash.

The fruits are a cluster of small pomes ranging in colour from sunshine yellow to vermilion. These are borne from the generous racemes of frothy white flowers, each bearing five petals and a delicate spray of twenty fimbriated stamens surrounding the ovary.

Hawthorn (*Crataegus* spp.)

Comprised of several dozen species, the hawthorn somewhat resembles its cousin the rowan, with its scrubby tree habit, delicate sprays of white, five-petalled blooms and preference for temperate climates. Its leaves are certainly different, though, deeply lobed and simple rather than compound. The stout thorns which give the plant its name are actually very short, sharp-tipped branches; they occasionally grow directly from the trunk of the tree. An Asian relative, the Indian hawthorn (*Rhaphiolepis* spp.), produces pink flowers and dark-blue fruits that can be turned into jam.

Blueberry and Kin (*Vaccinium* spp. &c.)

Like the rest of the members of the Ericaceae family (for example, rhododendron, heather, madrone, wintergreen and so on), the Vaccinia are best known for their little white or pink cup- or bell-shaped flowers and leathery, evergreen leaves. Some are scrubby and prostrate, others are bushy or like small, shrubby trees, and some, such as the strawberry tree (*Arbutus unedo* and *A. andrachne*), grow into full trees. Of the nine subfamilies of the Ericaceae, the Vaccinioideae contains the most commercially important genera: blueberries, huckleberries, cranberries, lingonberries and so on.

Gooseberries and Currants (*Ribes* spp.)

Currants and gooseberries are cosmopolitan, growing native all over Europe, North America, Asia and northwestern Africa. They grow in medium-sized bushes; the stems of currants are typically smooth, while gooseberries are covered in fine spines. Their fragrant flowers, typically pink, white or yellow, grow in pendent racemes.

Elderberry (*Sambucus* spp.)

These were once classified in the honeysuckle (Caprifoliaceae) family, but molecular data have recently slotted them, along with viburnums, into the moschatel (Adoxaceae) family. Arborescent elderberry shrubs grow in forest understoreys and on field edges.

Their leaves are pinnate and flimsy, and their flowers, typically open panicles of white or sometimes pink, are aromatic.

Mulberry (*Morus* spp.)

The mulberries represent a dozen or so species of typically deciduous trees, widespread throughout northern Africa, the Middle East, southern Europe and the Mediterranean, plus South Asia. The aggregates of juicy drupelets that somewhat resemble a blackberry are borne from very inconspicuous green flowers, the females of which are little more than ovaries with pistils sticking out like fuzzy white tongues. The male flowers are further reduced, consisting simply of wee stamens poking crudely out of sepals. However, they ejaculate their pollen at a speed of approximately 560 km/h (350 mph) – the fastest plant movement ever recorded.

Black Nightshade (*Solanum nigrum*, *S. retroflexum* and *S. scabrum*)

This weedy, herbaceous plant (which shares a genus with tomatoes and potatoes) grows about a metre tall, with simple, lobed leaves and little white flowers that point their yellow noses (anthers) downward, as the other members of its genus do. The berries are spherical, starting out bitter, green and inedible, and ripening to a purplish black. Fossil evidence from as early as the Palaeolithic suggests it may have been one of the plants inhabiting ancient England.

Goji Berry (*Lycium barbarum* and *L. chinense*)

Also representing the nightshade family, goji berries (also known as wolfberries) have been cultivated in China since at least the Shang Dynasty, approximately 4,000 years ago. Much as it is in Ningxia province of North China, where it's predominantly grown today, the plant is used in some coastal areas of Britain to reduce erosion and to prevent desert or dune soils from altering coastlines.

The plant grows up to about 3 m (11 ft) high, with a woody, vining stem, elongated leaves, purple-petalled nightshade flowers on slender pedicels and a slightly elongated vermilion berry.

Barberry (*Berberis vulgaris*)

The European barberry, a stout deciduous shrub growing up to 4 m (13 ft) high, runs wild throughout Europe and western Asia. The entire plant is sharp; its stems and leaves are covered in spines, and its red berry is acerbic with high levels of malic acid.

Once introduced to North America for food and ornamental qualities in the early 1600s, it spread so quickly that a national eradication programme was eventually launched for the species in the U.S. in 1918, and because it is a vector for wheatstem rust (a disease affecting cereal grasses), growing the species is banned outright in Canada.

Açaí (*Euterpe oleracea*)

Açaí 'berries' (actually drupes) are the fruits of a palm tree that grows in forested wetlands and rich floodplains in the Amazon and Trinidad.

The plants are much like any other palm tree: tall, slender, invoking images of tropical holidays. The fruits are about the size of a cherry or olive, and grow on long, branched panicles, as their cousins the dates do. Like all drupes, their fruit is fleshy with a hard seed; in this case, the flesh is dark purple and yields a thick brownish-purple pulp.

Honeyberry (*Lonicera caerulea*)

The edible blue honeysuckle, or haskap, grows wild in northern Japan, the subalpine forests of New England and northern and eastern Europe. The plant, which grows upwards of 2 m (6½ ft) tall, has woody stems and oval leaves growing in pairs. White, trumpet-shaped flowers appear in pairs in the spring. The fruits are about 1 cm (⅓ in) in diameter. Coinciding with the strawberry season, the dark-blue berries ripen in June. Honeyberry exhibits wide polymorphism in its fruits, a trait that perplexed botanists at the turn of the last century.

Although the berries are mostly indigo and roughly elongate, the fruit morphology of the plant is so diverse that no fewer than *nine* varieties of the species are recognized by botanists today. The berries can be nearly cylindrical with a blunt-flat end; they can be pear-shaped or look like miniature plums; they can be lumpy-ovate; they can be jaggedly asymmetrical or shaped like tiny cerulean bananas.

Miracle Fruit (*Synsepalum dulcificum*)

Miracle fruit is a West African species whose family includes the sapote fruit and the nut that produces shea butter. Miracle fruit is a tall, densely bushy evergreen shrub, producing white flowers and red berries that somewhat resemble coffee beans.

The fruit is only mildly sweet-tart, but contains a molecule called miraculin which binds to the taste buds and is triggered by low pH (high acidity) to activate the tongue's sugar receptors. Two other species are called 'miracle fruit', but only one has similar properties: *Thaumatococcus daniellii* (named after the previously mentioned Daniell). The fruit of this species, also West African and also a red berry (or more specifically, a berry-like aril), doesn't make sour foods taste sweet by tricking the tongue; it's 2,000 times sweeter than sugar.

Recipes

Historic Recipes

Gooseberry Fool

There are so many fool recipes out there, but this one from Eliza Leslie's *Directions for Cookery, in its Various Branches* (1837) does double duty as a pudding recipe, with the added instructions at the end. Using an entire nutmeg, however, might not be a good idea (unless a splitting headache is the desired result) – a quarter-teaspoon of freshly grated nutmeg should do the trick.

To Stew Gooseberries

Top and tail them. Pour some boiling water on the gooseberries, cover them up, and let them set about half an hour, or till the skin is quite tender, but not till it bursts, as that will make the juice run out into the water. Then pour off the water, and mix with the gooseberries an equal quantity of sugar. Put them into a porcelain stew-pan or skillet, and set it on hot coals, or on a charcoal furnace. In a few minutes you may begin to mash them against the side of the pan with a wooden spoon. Let them stew about half an hour, stirring them frequently. They must be quite cold before they are used for any thing.

Gooseberry Fool

Having stewed two quarts of gooseberries in the above manner, stir them as soon as they are cold into a quart of rich boiling milk. Grate in a nutmeg, and covering the pan, let the gooseberries simmer in the milk for five minutes. Then stir in the beaten yolks of two or three eggs, and immediately remove it from the fire. Keep on the cover a few minutes longer; then turn out the mixture into a deep dish or a glass bowl, and set it away to get cold, before it goes to table. Eat it with sponge-cake. It will probably require additional sugar.

Gooseberries prepared in this manner make a very good pudding, with the addition of a little grated bread. Use both whites and yolks of the eggs. Stir the mixture well, and bake it in a deep dish. Eat it cold, with sugar grated over it.

Strawberry Shortcake

Mrs. Lincoln's Boston Cook Book: What to Do and What Not to Do in Cooking (1884) published a recipe that quite resembles the modern strawberry shortcake, if one uses the right combination of baking 'Short Cakes, No. 1' with the assembly instructions for 'Strawberry Short Cake No. 2'. Her 'Short Cakes No. 2' recipe yields one large cake, and her 'Strawberry Short Cake No. 1' calls for pie crust instead of soft biscuits.

Short Cakes, No. 1

1 pint sifted flour.
½ teaspoonful salt, scant.
½ teaspoonful soda, measured after pulverizing.
1 full teaspoonful cream of tartar (omit if sour milk be used).
¼ cup butter.
1 cup sweet or sour milk, or cold water.

Mix the salt, soda, and cream of tartar with the flour, and sift two or three times. Rub in the butter until fine like meal, or if liked very short and crisp, melt the butter and add it hot with the milk. Add the liquid gradually, mixing and cutting with a knife, and use just enough to make it of a light spongy consistency. Scrape out the dough upon a well-floured board; toss it with the knife until floured; pat into a flat cake, and roll gently, till half an inch thick; cut with a small round cutter, and bake on the griddle or in the oven. If you use a griddle, grease it well with salt pork or butter, and cook the cakes slowly; watch and turn them, that all may be browned alike.

When they are well puffed up, put a bit of butter on the top of each, and turn over, – or move them to one side and grease again with the pork, and turn over upon the freshly greased place. When browned on the other side and done, of which you can judge by the firmness of texture or by pulling one partly open, serve immediately. Tear them open, as cutting with a knife makes them heavy and indigestible. If to be baked in the oven, put them quite close together in a shallow pan, and bake ten or fifteen minutes.

Short Cakes, No. 2

Make by rule No. 1 for Short Cake, and bake on a griddle in small rounds. Tear open, and spread each half with softened butter. Put half of the cakes on a hot plate. Mash a pint of strawberries, sweeten to taste, put a large spoonful on each cake; then put another layer of cakes, and whole berries, well sugared. Serve with cream.

Elderberry Wine

Hannah Glasse offers several recipes for berry wines in her *Art of Cookery* (1747), but her elderberry wine recipe actually makes a syrup intended to fortify one's raisin wine. Her use of flour, egg whites and fixed nitre (that is, saltpetre) are intended to flocculate the sediments to clarify the wine, but isinglass would also be effective.

Take elder-berries, when pretty ripe, plucked from the green stalks, what quantity you please, and press them that the juice may freely run from them, which may be done in a cyder-press, or between two weighty planks, or for want of this opportunity, you may mash them, and then it will run easily; put the juice in a well-seasoned cask, and to every barrel put three gallons of water strong of honey boiled in it, and add some ale yeast to make it ferment, and work out the grossness of its body; then to clarify it, add flour, whites of eggs, and a little fixed nitre; when it has well fermented and grows fine, draw it from the settlings, and keep it till spring; then to every barrel add five pounds of its own flowers, and as much loaf sugar, and let it stand seven days; at the end of which it will grow very rich, and have a good flavour.

Loganberry Dumplings

This recipe comes from *The Neighborhood Cook Book*, published in 1912 by the Council of Jewish Women in Portland, Oregon. At the time this book was published, loganberries had been in cultivation in Oregon, where they're still commercially grown, for only about a decade. The marionberry was still more than forty years away from invention. Any type of blackberry would do as a replacement for loganberries in this recipe, but an Oregon-grown variety would be ideal.

One quart loganberries cooked until soft and sweetened to taste, (or the same quantity of canned fruit). Dumplings. Two cups flour, one-half teaspoon salt, two heaping teaspoons Crescent baking powder sifted together twice. Add one beaten egg mixed with enough milk to absorb flour. Drop by tablespoonful on boiling fruit. Cover closely and cook gently for fifteen or twenty minutes. Serve in individual dishes with whipped cream.

Raspberry Vinegar

This drinking vinegar, one of several offered in Marion Harland's *Common Sense in the Household* (1884), is virtually identical to a shrub.

Put the raspberries into a stone vessel and mash them to a pulp. Add cider-vinegar – no specious imitation, but the genuine article – enough to cover it well. Stand in the sun twelve hours, and all night in the cellar. Stir up well occasionally during this time. Strain, and put as many fresh berries in the jar as you took out; pour the strained vinegar over them; mash and set in the sun all day. Strain a second time next day. To each quart of this juice allow

1 pint of water.
5 lbs. of sugar (best white) for every 3 pints of this liquid,
juice and water mingled.

Place over a gentle fire and stir until the sugar is dissolved. Heat slowly to boiling, skimming off the scum and as soon as it fairly boils take off and strain. Bottle while warm, and seal the corks with sealing-wax, or bees' wax and rosin.

A most refreshing and pleasant drink.

Tipparee Jelly

From the updated (1907) edition of *Mrs Beeton's Book of Household Management* comes this tipparee jelly, like those seen in cookbooks published for British housewives living in India during the British Raj.

Ingredients. – Tipparee pods (Cape gooseberries), sugar, lemon-juice
Method. – Wipe the pods, cover them with cold water, simmer gently until soft, then drain through a jelly bag, but do not squeeze the pulp. Measure the liquor; to each add 1 lb of sugar and 1 dessert-spoonful

of lemon-juice, and simmer gently for ½ an hour, skimming meanwhile. Pour the jelly into prepared moulds, or into jars if not required for immediate use.

Time. – About 2 hours. Average Cost, uncertain.

Pilāw, Persian Fashion

This recipe comes from Turabi Efendi's surprisingly discursive *Turkish Cookery Book* (1862). This pilaf is very similar to the Persian jewel rice served at weddings. Just use chicken instead of mutton, omit the pistachios and swap barberries for the currants to turn this into *zereshk pulow*.

Àjèm Pilāwi – Cut three pounds of nice mutton in pieces about the size of walnuts, place them in a stewpan: if the meat is not fat, add three or four ounces of fresh butter; put the pan on a charcoal fire, and let the meat stew till quite brown, but not burnt, and the fat is as clear as oil, which you will easily see by holding the pan on one side; then take out the pieces of meat with a hand strainer, and put them in a basin; then put three or four finely chopped onions in the remaining fat, and fry them a nice brown; then lay the pieces of meat over, add one or two handfuls of pistachios, the same of currants, a teaspoonful of mixed spice, two pounds of the best rice, well washed, pour gently two quarts of cold water over, add sufficient salt, put the cover over the pan, and cement round it with flour paste, so as to keep the steam in, put the pan on the fire, and let it boil gently until the whole of the liquid is absorbed; then take off the cover, and turn the contents of the pan carefully on to a hot dish, and serve.

This Pilāwi is very pleasing to the sight, and exceedingly pleasant to the palate.

Modern Recipes

Blackcurrant Jam

The rock band Grizzly Bear declares blackcurrant jam as the zenith
of all preserves, and having a bit of this on a warm, buttered scone,
one is wont to agree with them. With so much natural pectin in currants, this jam is easy to make, and would be delightful in a roly-poly.

1 lb (½ kg) blackcurrants, stems removed
1 cup (240 ml) water
2¼ cups (½ kg) sugar
1 tbsp crème de cassis (optional)

Put the currants in a heavy-bottomed pot, cover with water and bring
to a boil. Turn the heat down to medium low and simmer for about
15–20 minutes or until the currants are quite soft and the liquid is
nearly evaporated. Mash them with a potato masher or the back of a
wooden spoon, stir in the sugar and crème de cassis, and cook for five
more minutes until the jam passes the 'nudge test' (drip a little onto
an ice-cold plate; if it wrinkles when nudged, it's ready). Ladle into
sterilized jars, wipe the rims with a hot washcloth, then tightly affix
the lids. Allow to cool completely before refrigerating, or process
in a boiling water bath for ten minutes to make the jars shelf-stable.
Makes approximately 600 ml or a few jam jars' worth

Blueberry Yoghurt Coffee Cake

Nothing beats warm coffee cake on a Sunday morning, except for
warm blueberry coffee cake with a crunchy topping. This recipe is
loosely adapted from *The Joy of Cooking*, by combining their sour
cream coffeecake and blueberry crunch coffeecake recipes.

¼ cup (30 g) sliced almonds
¼ cup (50 g) brown sugar
½ tsp cinnamon

1 ¾ cups (210 g) all-purpose plain flour
⅔ cup (130 g) sugar
1 tbsp baking powder
1 tbsp baking soda
½ tsp salt
1 tsp lemon zest
a few good scratches of fresh nutmeg (or ¼ tsp ground)
5 tbsp (70 g) cold unsalted butter, cut into pieces
1 large egg
¾ cup (175 ml) full-fat yoghurt (or sour cream)
1 tsp vanilla
1 cup (150 g) fresh or frozen blueberries, tossed in a tsp
of flour to coat

Preheat oven to 180°C (350°F). Grease a 6-cup loaf pan (21 × 11 × 6 cm or 8.5 × 4.5 × 2.5 in.); lining the pan with a strip of baking paper will also help release the loaf. Mix the almonds, brown sugar and cinnamon, and spread them in the bottom of the loaf pan.

Place the dry ingredients and lemon zest in a food processor and pulse a couple times to mix. Add the butter, pulsing again a few times until the butter is cut in and the mix resembles coarse crumbs, taking care not to overdo it. (This can also be done with a fork or pastry cutter).

In a separate large bowl, mix the yoghurt, egg and vanilla until thoroughly combined, and then stir the flour mixture into the wet ingredients. Fold in the berries until evenly distributed, and then spread the batter into the loaf pan. Bake for 55–60 minutes, or until a toothpick inserted in the centre comes out clean. (Note: baking time will increase by about 5–10 minutes if using frozen berries).

Allow to cool in the pan on a rack for 10–15 minutes, then run a knife along the edges to loosen, and invert onto a rack to finish cooling. The sliced almonds and brown sugar will have formed a crunchy caramel topping on the coffee cake. It can be served warm, but if you allow it to cool completely before diving in, your patience will be rewarded with a crunchier topping.

Serves 8–10

Cranberry Sauce

Eliza Leslie's straightforward recipe calls simply for cranberries, water and brown sugar, and yields a perfectly serviceable sauce. This recipe is only slightly more embellished but, with roast turkey, is just as delicious.

1 12-oz (340 g) bag of fresh or frozen cranberries
1 cup (200 g) sugar
¾ cup (180 ml) water
zest and juice of 1 orange

Bring all the ingredients to a boil, and then simmer over a low heat, stirring occasionally until the berries pop open. Mash them to the desired texture; using a potato masher gives a chunkier, chutney-like texture, and using an immersion blender gives a smoother, jelly-like consistency.

Makes about 500 ml (1 pint)

Pickled Gooseberries

Originally made to serve with smoked mackerel, these go well with any other oily fish or fatty meat. They're outstanding with a dish of hot-smoked trout and grilled plums, or with meats, cheeses and other pickles, in a fancier version of a ploughman's lunch.

1 pint (300 g) fresh gooseberries, washed and picked over to remove stems
1 cup (240 ml) white vinegar
1 tbsp white sugar
¼ tsp kosher (sea) salt
2 cloves
3 allspice berries
¼ tsp peppercorns
¼ tsp white mustard seeds
½ a thinly sliced shallot

Place gooseberries in a clean pint or half-litre jar. Warm the remaining ingredients until the sugar and salt dissolve, and then pour over the gooseberries. It's fine to dump any excess brine; just make sure the spices end up in the jar. Refrigerate for at least a week, preferably a month.

Makes about 500 ml (1 pint)

Chinese Herbal Black Chicken Soup (*Wu Gu Ji Tong*)

In Chinese households, this soup is part of the traditional month-long 'confinement diet' fed to new mothers right after giving birth. However, this soup can be enjoyed by anyone. An ordinary chicken can be used if black-skinned silkies aren't available, but the rest of the ingredients should be available at Asian groceries.

1 whole silkie chicken (about 2–2½ lbs or 1 kg), head and feet removed
½ cup (120 ml) Shaoxing rice wine (not cooking wine)
1 5-cm (2-in.) piece of ginger, peeled and thinly sliced
½ cup (50 g) goji berries (aka wolfberries)
½ cup (50 g) pitted jujubes (aka red dates)
4 large or 8 small dried scallops, rinsed
2 cloud ear mushrooms (Chinese black fungus), rinsed
salt
1 spring onion (scallion), thinly sliced on the bias

Cut the chicken into eight pieces, leaving the bones in. In a large stockpot, cover the chicken with water. Boil for two minutes, and then remove the chicken and set aside. This was just a cleansing bath, so dump the water and rinse out the pot. Return the chicken to the pot and add 3½ quarts (3.3 l) of water and the rice wine.

Put the ginger, goji berries, jujubes, scallops and mushrooms in a large Chinese medicine filter bag (available in Asian grocery stores or tea shops) or tie them in a cheesecloth – this is so they can be easily retrieved when straining the broth. Add this to the stockpot with the chicken. Bring back up to a boil and skim the scum from the surface. Turn down the heat and simmer for an hour or so, until the chicken is nearly falling off the bone.

Carefully remove the chicken pieces to a large serving bowl with a strainer spoon, and then add the contents of the tea bag or cheesecloth (you can thinly slice the mushrooms now that they're softened up – just remove the stem first). Put the filter bag or cheesecloth in a colander and pour the stock through (into the serving bowl) to strain it thoroughly. Add salt to taste, and then top the soup with the sliced spring onions.

Serves 8

Blueberry-Elderflower Daiquiri

Blueberries and elderflower pair remarkably well. This cocktail was inspired by a huckleberry daiquiri served once upon a time at the historic Multnomah Falls Lodge in Oregon, but here we've added elderflower liqueur for a touch of floral sweetness. We've omitted the Lodge's unnecessary whipped cream topping.

1 cup (150 g) frozen blueberries
3 oz (90 ml) light or golden rum (not spiced rum)
2 tbsp fresh lemon juice
2 tbsp elderflower liqueur or cordial (St-Germain or Flädersaft are fine)
2 cups ice

Frappé all ingredients in a blender until smooth, and then pour into glasses.

Serves 2

References

1 Botany

1 Henry Nicholson Ellacombe, *The Plant-lore and Garden-craft of Shakespeare* (London, 1884), p. 283.
2 Fredrik Wilhelm Christian Areschoug, *Some Observations on the Genus 'Rubus'* (Lund, Sweden, 1885), p. 1.
3 Pliny the Elder, *Natural History*, Book XXIII, at http://penelope.uchicago.edu, accessed 11 November 2016.
4 Richard Jefferies, *Nature Near London* (London, 1883), p. 201.
5 James Vick, *Vick's Monthly Magazine*, XI (1888), p. 94.
6 Jessup Whitehead, *The Steward's Handbook and Guide to Party Catering* (Chicago, IL, 1889), p. 332.
7 United States Department of Agriculture, 'Report of the Pomologist', *Yearbook of Agriculture* (Washington, DC, 1889), p. 593.
8 E. R. Root, ed., 'Wonderberry – Still More About It', *Gleanings in Bee Culture*, XXXVII (1909), p. 719.
9 Ying Wang et al., 'Chemical and Genetic Diversity of Wolfberry', in *Lycium Barbarum and Human Health* (Dordrecht, 2015), p. 2.
10 Frank D. Kern, 'Observations of the Dissemination of the Barberry', *Ecology*, 3 (July 1921), p. 212.
11 John Good, Esq., *Pantologia: A New Cabinet Cyclopaedia, Comprehending a Complete Series of Essays, Treatises, and Systems, Alphabetically Arranged* (London, 1819), vol. IV, p. 8.

12 William F. Daniell, 'On the *Synsepalum dulcificum, De Cand.*; or, Miraculous Berry of Western Africa', *Pharmaceutical Journal*, XI (1852), pp. 445–6.

2 Berry-lore

1 Elias Lönnrot and John Martin Crawford, trans., *The Kalevala* (New York, 1888), pp. 720–22.

2 Percy Stafford Allen and John de Monins Johnson, *Transactions of the Third International Congress for the History of Religions: Religions of the Lower Culture. Section II. Religions of China and Japan. Section III. Religions of the Egyptians. Section IV. Religions of the Semites* (Oxford, 1908), p. 80.

3 Ibid., p. 511.

4 Edmund Leamy, *Irish Fairy Tales* (Dublin, 1890), p. 89.

5 Maud Grieve, *A Modern Herbal: The Medicinal, Culinary, Cosmetic and Economic Properties, Cultivation and Folk-lore of Herbs, Grasses, Fungi, Shrubs, and Trees with All Their Modern Scientific Uses* (New York, 1931), vol. II, p. 585.

6 Ibid.

7 Jeremy Taylor, *The Works of Jeremy Taylor*, vol. V (London, 1831), p. 366.

8 Richard Folkard, *Plant Lore, Legends, and Lyrics: Embracing the Myths, Traditions, Superstitions, and Folk-lore of the Plant Kingdom* (London, 1884), p. 259.

9 Ibid.

10 C. A. Willard, 'The History of Some of Our Cultivated Fruits', *Transactions of the Wisconsin State Horticultural Society*, XVII (1887), p. 68.

11 Phil Robinson, *The Poets' Birds* (London, 1873), p. 396.

12 Charlotte Sophia Burne, *The Handbook of Folklore* (London, 1914), p. 34.

13 Ossian, 'The Pursuit of Diarmuid O'Duibhne and Gráinne, the Daughter of Cormac', *Transactions of the Ossianic Society*, III (1857), p. 119.

3 Picking and Growing

1 Hezekiah G. Wells, *Report of the Secretary of the Michigan State Board of Agriculture* (Lansing, MI, 1880), p. 131.

2 Joseph Henry Maiden, *The Useful Native Plants of Australia (Including Tasmania)* (Sydney, 1889), p. 1.

3 William Curtis, Samuel Curtis, Joseph-Dalton Hooker, William Jackson Hooker and John Sims, 'Billardiera Scandens, Climbing Billardiera, or Apple-berry', *The Botanical Magazine: Or, Flower Garden Displayed Etc.*, XXI (1805), p. 801.

4 Herbert O. Lang, *History of the Willamette Valley, Being a Description of the Valley and its Resources, With an Account of its Discovery and Settlement by White Men, and its Subsequent History: Together with Personal Reminiscences of its Early Pioneers* (Portland, OR, 1885), p. 570.

5 Samuel Carson, 'Camping in Mendocino', *Overland Monthly* (San Francisco, CA) (October 1893), p. 345.

6 Rebecca Richards and Susan Alexander, USDA Forest Service, *A Social History of Wild Huckleberry Harvesting in the Pacific Northwest* (Portland, OR, 2006), p. 16.

7 Charles Dickens, 'A Cow-brute Tragedy', *All the Year Round: A Weekly Journal* (21 April 1894), pp. 368–71.

8 Ibid.

9 'Guide to Cloudberries', *My Little Norway*, http://mylittlenorway.com, 19 July 2011.

10 Lang, *History of the Willamette Valley*, p. 570.

11 Ibid.

12 Col. W. Rhodes, 'The Culture of the Strawberry Plant in the District of Quebec', *Annual Report of the Montreal Horticultural Society and Fruit Growers' Association in Quebec* (1885), p. 44.

13 George M. Darrow, *Strawberry: History, Breeding, Physiology* (New York, 1966), p. 12.

14 Richard Gay Pardee, *A Complete Manual for the Cultivation of the Strawberry: With a Description of the Best Varieties. Also, Notices of the Raspberry, Blackberry, Currant, Gooseberry, and Grape; with Directions for Their Cultivation, and Selection of the Best Varieties* (New York, 1854), p. vii.

15 Luther Burbank, 'Heredity', *Gardening*, 13 (1905), p. 178.

16 Advertisement for Stingley Brothers farm in *Polk County Observer* (Monmouth, OR) (13 June 1913), p. 6.

17 'Preparation and Work for the Berry Season: Good Fruit Brings Good Prices', *American Agriculturist*, 36 (1877), p. 178.

18 John Sammon, 'Driscoll's Growers Gave Former Interned Japanese Americans a Start', *Nikkei West*, 2011, www.nikkeiwest.com, accessed 11 November 2016.

19 Stephanie Strom, 'Driscoll's Aims to Hook the Berry-buying Shopper', *New York Times* (6 September 2016).

4 Dishes and Drinks

1 Marion Harland, *Common Sense in the Household* (New York, 1884), p. 444.

2 Ibid.

3 Ibid.

4 Edmund Spenser, 'Amoretti, Sonnet LXIV', *The Poetical Works of Edmund Spenser* (London, 1839), vol. V, p. 152.

5 Apicius, *De re coquinaria,* trans. Joseph Dommers Vehling, www.gutenberg.org, accessed 21 October 2016.

6 Magnus Nilsson, *The Nordic Cookbook* (London, 2015), p. 636.

7 Donna Light, 'CAMPUS LIFE: Middlebury; It All Started With Pie Tins in the Air', *New York Times* (9 July 1989).

8 Ibid.

9 Ibid.

10 Mary Johnson Bailey Lincoln, *Mrs. Lincoln's Boston Cook Book: What to Do and What Not to Do in Cooking* (Boston, MA, 1884), p. 85.

11 William Safire, 'Essay; Bagels vs. Doughnuts', www. nytimes.com, 25 October 1999.

12 Susan Coolidge, *Eyebright: A Story* (Boston, MA, 1879), p. 156.

13 Elizabeth Smith, *The Compleat Housewife; or, Accomplished Gentlewoman's Companion* (London, 1727), p. 191.

14 Rebecca Moore, 'Drinking the Kool-Aid: The Cultural Transformation of a Tragedy', http://jonestown.sdsu.edu, accessed 3 November 2016.

15 Heather Arndt Anderson, *Portland: A Food Biography* (Lanham, MD, 2014), p. 209.

16 Patrick Roper, 'Chequers Ale Lives Again', http://rowanswhitebeamsandservicetrees.blogspot.com, 4 March 2010.

17 Pierre Deleschamps, *Livre du brasseur, guide complet de la fabrication de la bière* (Paris, 1828), p. 102.

18 Carolyn Johnston Pouncy, *The 'Domostroi': Rules for Russian Households in the Time of Ivan the Terrible* (New York, 2014), pp. 197–8.

19 Peter Jonas, *The Distiller's Guide: Comprehending the Whole Art of Distillation and Rectification, in All Its Various Branches* (London, 1818), front cover.

20 H. Lintot, *A Compleat Body of Distilling: Explaining the Mysteries of that Science, in a Most Easy and Familiar Manner; Containing an Exact and Accurate Method of Making All the Compound Cordial-waters Now in Use* (London, 1731), p. 21.

21 Ibid.

22 Samuel Morewood, *A Philosophical and Statistical History of the Inventions and Customs of Ancient and Modern Nations in the Manufacture and Use of Inebriating Liquors* (Dublin, 1838), p. 513.

23 Jerry Thomas, *How to Mix Drinks; or, The Bon-vivant's Companion* (New York, 1862), p. 47.

24 Ibid.

5 Poison and Panacea

1 Charles John Samuel Thompson, *Poison Romance and Poison Mysteries* (London, 1899), p. 60.

2 John Wilkes, ed., *Encyclopaedia Londinensis; or, Universal Dictionary of Arts, Sciences, and Literature*, vol. xx (London, 1825), p. 823.

3 Sir Robert Christison, *A Treatise on Poisons in Relation to Medical Jurisprudence, Physiology and the Practice of Physic* (Edinburgh, 1835), p. 763.

4 Ibid.

5 J. U. and C. G. Lloyd, 'Mr Cutler's Account of Indigenous Vegetables, Botanically Arranged', *Bulletin of the Lloyd Library of Botany, Pharmacy and Materia Medica* (1903), p. 455.

6 Hannah Glasse and Maria Wilson, *The Complete Confectioner; or, Housekeeper's Guide: to a Simple and Speedy Method of Understanding the Whole Art of Confectionary* (London, 1800), p. 274.

7 Ibid., pp. 272–3.

8 Martin Blochwich, *Anatomia Sambuci; or, the Anatomie of the Elder, Etc.* (London, 1677), front cover.

9 'Schisandra: Ultimate Superberry', www.medicinehunter. com, accessed 9 November 2016.

10 B. L. Beyerstein, 'Alternative Medicine and Common Errors of Reasoning', *Academic Medicine*, LXXVI/3 (2001), pp. 230–37.

11 E. N. Anderson, *Everyone Eats: Understanding Food and Culture*, 2nd edn (New York, 2014), pp. 69–70.

Appendix

1 Stark Bros website, 'Kiowa Berry', www.starkbros.com, accessed 11 November 2016.

2 Karl McKay Wiegand, 'The Genus Amelanchier in Eastern North America', in *Rhodora* (Boston, MA, 1921), p. 117.

3 Ibid., p. 118.

4 Harry F. Clements, 'Morphology and Physiology of the Pome Lenticels of *Pyrus Malus*', *Botanical Gazette*, XCVII/1 (September 1935), p. 101.

Bibliography

Berzok, Linda Murray, *American Indian Food* (Westport, CT, 2005)

Blochwich, Martin, *Anatomia Sambuci; or, the Anatomie of the Elder* (London, 1677)

Bowling, Barbara L., *The Berry Grower's Companion* (Portland, OR, 2000)

Brown, Catherine, *A Year in a Scot's Kitchen* (Glasgow, 1996)

Darrow, George McMillan, *The Strawberry: History, Breeding, and Physiology* (New York, 1966)

Eck, Paul, *The American Cranberry* (New Brunswick, NJ, 1990)

Edmonds, Jennifer M., and James A. Chweya, *Black Nightshades: Solanum Nigrum L. and Related Species* (Rome, 1997)

Folkard, Richard, *Plant Lore, Legends, and Lyrics: Embracing the Myths, Traditions, Superstitions, and Folk-lore of the Plant Kingdom* (London, 1884)

Forsell, Mary, and Tony Cenicola, *Berries: Cultivation, Decoration, and Recipes* (New York, 1989)

Fuller, Andrew, *The Small Fruit Culturist* (New York, 1867)

Gunther, Erna, *Ethnobotany of Western Washington* (Seattle, WA, 1945)

Gupta, Ramesh C., ed., *Nutraceuticals: Efficacy, Safety and Toxicity* (London, 2016)

Hancock, J. F., *Strawberries* (New York, 1999)

Hibler, Janie, *The Berry Bible: With 175 Recipes Using Cultivated and Wild, Fresh and Frozen Berries* (New York, 2004)

Holmes, Roger, *Taylor's Guide to Fruits and Berries* (Boston, MA, 1996)

Jennings, Jay, *Knott's Berry Farm: The Early Years* (Charleston, NC, 2009)

Kloet, S. P. Vander, *The Genus Vaccinium in North America* (Ottowa, 1988)

Lloyd, T. Abe, and Fiona Hamersley Chambers, *Wild Berries of Washington and Oregon* (Auburn, WA, 2014)

Moerman, Daniel, *Native American Ethnobotany* (Portland, OR, 1998)

Richards, Rebecca, and Susan Alexander, *A Social History of Wild Huckleberry Harvesting in the Pacific Northwest* (Portland, OR, 2006)

Seymour, Tom, *Foraging New England: Edible Wild Food and Medicinal Plants from Maine to the Adirondacks to Long Island Sound* (Lanham, MD, 2013)

Smith, Jane, *The Garden of Invention: Luther Burbank and the Business of Breeding Plants* (London, 2009)

Watson, W.C.R., *Handbook of the Rubi of Great Britain and Ireland* (Cambridge, 1958)

Websites and Associations

Cooking

British Society of Baking
http://britishsocietyofbaking.org.uk

European Association of Fruit and Vegetable Processors
www.profel-europe.eu

European Confederation of Bakers and
Confectionary Organizations
www.cebp.eu

Food in Jars
http://foodinjars.com

National Center for Home Food Preservation
http://nchfp.uga.edu

The Guild of Jam and Preserve Makers
www.jamguild.co.uk

Growing

The Blackcurrant Foundation
www.blackcurrantfoundation.co.uk

British Summer Fruits
www.britishsummerfruits.co.uk

Driscoll's
www.driscolls.com

International Society for Horticultural Science
www.ishs.org

Naturipe Farms
www.naturipefarms.com

North American Raspberry and Blackberry Association
www.raspberryblackberry.com

North American Strawberry Growers Association
www.nasga.org

Ontario Berry Growers Association
http://ontarioberries.com

Oregon Raspberry and Blackberry Commission
www.oregon-berries.com

Wild Blueberries of North America
www.wildblueberries.com

Wild Huckleberry Association
http://wildhuckleberry.com

Research

Cornell University Fruit Resources
www.fruit.cornell.edu

EU Berry Project
www.euberry.univpm.it

Journal of Berry Research
www.iospress.nl

North Willamette Research and Extension Center, Oregon
State University
http://oregonstate.edu/dept/NWREC

Saskatoon Berry Institute
http://saskatoonberryinstitute.org

United States Department of Agriculture PLANTS Database
http://plants.usda.gov

Acknowledgements

Thanks go out to all the researchers bridging the gap between science and agriculture so that we have so many nice things to eat. I'd also like to thank Luther Burbank, who filled the world with his beautiful, useful, 'strange freaks'.

And I thank The Whom. I can't believe you all have let me tag around this long.

Photo Acknowledgements

The author and publishers wish to express their thanks to the below sources of illustrative material and/or permission to reproduce it. (Some information not included in the captions for reasons of brevity is also given below.)

Photos by or courtesy of the author: pp. 11, 59, 74, 87, 91, 94, 103, 106, 107, 113, 127; Bibliothèque Nationale de France, Paris: p. 60 (Ms Latin 1156B); from I. J. Bilibin, □□□□□□ (Folk-Tales) (St Petersburg, 1903): p. 31; from Elizabeth Blackwell, *A Curious Herbal, containing Five Hundred Cuts, of the most Useful Plants . . .* (London, 1737): p. 13 (photo u.s. National Library of Medicine Digital Collections); from [Randolph Caldecott], *The Complete Collection of Pictures and Songs by Randolph Caldecott* (London, 1887): p. 38 (photo Library of Congress, Washington, DC); photo David Castor: p. 84; from *Complimentary Banquet Given by the California State Board of Trade In Honor of Luther Burbank at the Palace Hotel, San Francisco, September 14th, 1903* (n.p., n.d. [San Francisco, 1903]): p. 62 (photo Library of Congress); photo Edward S. Curtis/Library of Congress, Washington, DC: p. 30 (Edward S. Curtis Collection); photo Didgeman: p. 85; photo Lorenz Frølich: p. 41; photo Ela Haney: p. 99; photo Lewis Wicks Hine/Library of Congress, Washington, DC (Prints and Photographs Division): p. 66; photo from the Knott's Berry Farm Collection, courtesy of Orange County Archives: p. 70; from *The Ladies' Home Journal*, LXV/2 (February 1948): p. 82 (photo Janice Bluestein Longone Culinary Archive); photo Russell Lee/Library of Congress, Washington,

Index

italic numbers refer to illustrations; **bold** to recipes

7-Eleven 74, 99

açaí (*Euterpe oleracea*) 23, 107,
    129, 136
amla 75, *76*, 80
amulets 27–8
anthocyanin 128
Apicius (book) 75, 109
arraki 110–11
artificial flavour 73–5, 98
Australia 48–9, *49*

Bakewell pudding 87
Bakewell tart 87
baneberry 120–21
barberry (*Berberis* spp.) 10,
    22–3, *23*, 75–6, *77*, 80, 104,
    136, 144
Bar-le-Duc jelly 84–5
Beeton, Isabella 80, 86–7,
    92–3, 143
belladonna 21, 36, 119–20, *122*
berry bowl 72
beverages 17, 104–15, 141,
    143, 149

beer/ale 17, 107–9
cordials 112
juice 91, 105–6, *106*
soda 106–7
spirits 110–11
tea 78, 105, 110
wine 109–10, 141
bilberry 10, 16, *18*, 28, 52, 55,
    77, 79, 89, 104, 125, 129
blåbärssoppa (bilberry soup)
    104
blackberry 12–13, 27, 28, *62*,
    63–4, 79, *82*, 89, 102, *102*,
    109–10, 112, 132, 142
breeding 59–64
growing 47, 57–9
folklore 28–9, 37, *38*
medicine 121, 123, *124*,
    129
picking 47, 49
'Blackcurrant Jam' (song) 121
Blackcurrant Jam **145**
blue honeysuckle *see*
    honeyberry
blue raspberry 73–4, *74*, 107

blueberry 10, 16–17, 24, 28,
    52, 58, 68, *77*, 88–9, *91*,
    134
    bagel 99
    Blueberry-Elderflower
    Daiquiri **149**
    Blueberry Yoghurt Coffee
    Cake **145–6**
    bun 99
    growing 58, 68
    muffin 99–100, *99*
    pancake 100
botany 9–25, 130–37
boysenberry 13, 61, 70, 132
bramble (*Rubus* spp.) 11,
    12–13, 57–8, *59*, 102, *102*,
    132
    botany 12–13, 132
    see also individual species/
    varieties
brandy 110
bread-and-butter berry *see*
    hawthorn
breeding 59–62, 68–70
    see also Burbank, Luther
Burbank, Luther 62–4, *62*, *63*

Canada 17, 45, 51, 83, *88*, 90
caneberry *see* bramble
cape gooseberry (*Physalis* spp.)
    56, *56*, 80
Chambord 112
chequer *see* rowan
China 21, 42–3, 55, 68, 101–2,
    109, 126–9, 135
    Chinese Herbal Black
    Chicken Soup **148–9**

Christians 27–8, 33
cloudberry 12, 52, 55, *57*, 77–8,
    112
cobbler (cocktail) 114
cobbler (dish) 90
cocktails *106*, 113–15, *113*, *114*,
    149
confection 101–3, *102*, *103*
cranberry 10, 16–17, 30, *65*, *77*,
    79, 134, 147
    juice 91, 105, *106*
    sauce 17, 83, **147**
crisp (crumble) 90, *91*
crostata 86
crowberry (*Empetrum nigrum*)
    17
cultivation 47, 56–61
    see also Burbank, Luther
currant (*Ribes* spp.) 10, 18–19,
    76, 79–80, *85*, 92–3, 103,
    113, 134, 144, 145
    cassis 109, 112, *113*
    dried 92–3
    jelly 79, 83–6, 95
    medicinal uses 121,
    123–5
custard 87, 95

Dame Elder 38–40, *39*
Darrow, George 58, 68–70
De re coquinaria see Apicius
death 36–9, 41, 43, 44, 104–5,
    117
    berries as symbols or
    omens of 28, 36–7
    use of berries in
    graveyards 36, 38

dewberry 12, 110, 132
Domostroy (book) 105, 109
Driscoll's 67–8
drying 19, 21, 51, 76, *77*, 92,
    102, 110, 128
dumplings 93–5, 142
dwale *see* nightshade

elder (*Sambucus* spp.) 10,
    19–20, *19*, 28, 109–10,
    134
    Elderberry Wine **141–2**
    folklore 37–40, *39*
    medicinal uses 124–5
Elder Mother *see* Dame
    Elder
England *see* UK
Eton Mess 97
Everyman's Rights 54–5

fairies 28, 37, 40
    fairy tales 29–33
femininity, berries as symbols
    of 45, 73, 98
Finland 24, 26, 29, 52, 54–5,
    78, 104, 112
    see also Sami
First Fruits festival 51
five-flavour berry (*Schisandra
    chinensis*) 127–8
folklore 26–33
    Celtic 28, 32–3
    Chinese 42–3
    Gaelic 28, 40, 41
    German 32, 37, 39
    Greek 29
    Japanese 43

Jewish 36, 38
Native American 27, 43–6
Nordic 26, 29–30, 38, 40,
    41, *41*
Russian 30–32, *31*
fool 95, **139–40**

garden huckleberry *see*
    nightshade (black)
Glasse, Hannah 79–80, 95,
    109, 123, 125, 141
goji 10, 21, *77*, 127, 135–6,
    148–9
goldenberry *see* cape
    gooseberry
gooseberry (*Ribes uva-crispa*)
    10, 18–19, 72, 79, *81*, 83,
    95, 102, 134
    Gooseberry Fool
    139–40
    'hops' made from 72,
    102
    Pickled Gooseberries
    147–8
ground cherry *see* cape
    gooseberry

Harland, Marion 72–3, 143
haskap *see* honeyberry
hawthorn (*Crataegus* spp.)
    15–16, *16*, 101–2, 109,
    133–4
    in medicine 126–7, *126*,
    129
Himbeergeist 110
Holda *see* Dame Elder
holly (*Ilex* spp.) 27, 117, *119*

honeyberry (*Lonicera caerulea*)
    22, 24, 54, 111, 136–7
huckleberry 10, 16–17, 45, 58,
    134
    cake 100–101
    importance to Native
        Americans 49–52
Huckleberry Finn 58
Huckleberry Hound 58

India 19, 21, 36, 75, 80, 128,
    143–4
    see also amla, tipparee
Indian gooseberry (*Phylanthus
    emblica*) 75, *76*, 80

jam 15, 77–83, 86, 93, 99, 121,
    134, 145
    smash (cocktail) 114
Japan 12, *23*, 24, 43, 54, 67–8,
    129, 136
Jell-O *94*, 95–6
jelly 15, 79–80, 83–5
Jews 36, 38, 93, 99, 142
Jonestown Massacre 104–5
juice 91, 105–6, *106*
juneberry *see* serviceberry
juniper 10, 110

Kalevala (poem) 26
kir royale 112, *113*
kissel 78–9, *79*
Knott's Berry Farm 68–71,
    70
kompot (drink) 105–6
Kool-Aid 104–5
Korea 55, 109

lambic 108–9
lingonberry 10, 16, 19, 26, 52,
    55, 77–8, 80, 83, *84*, 100,
    105, 134
Linzertorte 86
Locusta 118–19
loganberry 12, 64, 93, 107,
    110, 132
    breeding 59–62
    Loganberry Dumplings
        142

mandrake 35–6, *35*
Manischewitz 110
marionberry 13, 61, 142
May tree *see* hawthorn
medicine 17, 58, 121–9, *123*, *126*
    Traditional Chinese
        Medicine (TCM) 126–8,
        148–9
Mediterranean 20, 21, 75, 135
    see also Ottoman
Metamorphosis (poem) 43
Mexico 68
Michaelmas 28–9
Middle East 20, 104, 111, 135
    see also Ottoman
miracle fruit (*Synsepalum
    dulcificum*) 24–5, 137
mors 105
mountain ash *see* rowan
mulberry (*Morus* spp.) 10, 20,
    42–3, 48, 75–6, *77*, 80, 109,
    112, 121, 135

Native Americans 17, 44–6,
    49–52, 121

New England 24, 89–90, 100–101, 136
nightshade (*Solanum* spp.) 21, 33–7, *34*, 93, 117–18, *118*, 135–6
    black 21, 93
    deadly *118*
    effects of 33–6
    see also belladonna, mandrake
Norway *18*, 52, 55, 77
nutritional supplements *127*, 128–9
nutraceuticals 128–9

Ocean Spray company 105
olallieberry 12, 61
Oregon grape 22, 49–50
Ottomans 75–6, 80, 104, 144

pectin 17, 19, 79–80, 145
Peru *23*, 56, 80
physalis *see* cape gooseberry
phytochemicals 128
picking *31*, 47–55, *65*
    by indigenous people 47–52, *50*, *53*
    child labour, use of 65–7, *66*
    hobby, as 52–5
    'U-Pick' 64–5
    use in fairy tales 29–32, *31*
    wild berries 47–55, *48*, *61*
pickle 75–6, *76*, 147–8
pie 88–90, *88*
    hand pie 88–9

pilaf 75–6
    Pilaw, Persian Fashion **144**
Pliny the Elder 15, 29, 58, 75
poison 36, 116–21, *117–19*, *122*
    Aqua Tofana 120
    see also Locusta (of Gaul), nightshade
Pop Tart 88
preserves 76–85
pudding 76, *78*, 87, 90–93, *92*, 139–40
    jam roly-poly
    spotted dick 92–3
    summer 92, *92*

raka 111
raspberry 12–13, *13*, 54, 61, *69*, 73–4, *77*, 79, 86, 89, 102, *102*, 104, 132
    beverages 108–10, 112
    blue 73–4, *74*, 107
    folklore 29–30
    medicine 125, 129
Raspberry Vinegar **143**
rowan (*Sorbus* spp.) 11, 14–15, *14*, 27, 32, 103, 108–9, 133
    folklore 40–41, *41*
Russia 7, 21, 24, 78, 91, 103, 105, 111
    fairy tales 30–32, *31*
    Germans from 21, 93

salal (*Gaultheria shallon*) 16–17
salmonberry 12, 51
Sami (people) 52

Saskatoon *see* serviceberry
Schwartzbeeren see nightshade,
    black
sea buckthorn (*Hippophae* spp.)
    77, 121, *123*, 128
service tree *see* rowan
serviceberry (*Amelanchier*
    spp.) 11, 13–14, 44, *88*, 90,
    132–3
shadberry *see* serviceberry
sherbet 104
shrub 104, 113–14, 143
Simmons, Amelia 23, 83
smoothie 105
soda 106–7
sorbet *see* sherbet
spotted dick 92–3
squash (drink) 104
strawberry (*Fragaria* spp.)
    9–12, *11*, 49, *60*, *61*, 72, 78,
    88–9, 93, *98*, 101
    artificial flavour/scent
    (furaneol) 73, 75, 98
    beverages 104, 107, 108,
    109–10, 112
    botany 9, 10, 131
    folklore 37, 45
    growing 58–9, 67–8
    medicinal use 121, 129
    shortcake (food) 96–7,
    98, **140–41**
    symbolism 37, 45, 73,
    98
strawberry delight 96
Strawberry Shortcake (doll)
    97–8
sunberry *see* nightshade, black

symbolism 27–8, 36, 46, 73, 98
syrup 40, 73, 85, 104, 113–14,
    123, 125, 141

tanghulu 126, *126*
tart 86–8
tea 78, 105, 110
tipparee 80
    Tipparee Jelly **143–4**
Traditional Chinese Medicine
    (TCM) 126–8, 148–9
trifle 95

UK 12, 17, 19–21, 29, 37, 59,
    76, 80, 83, 90, 92–3, 104,
    107–9, 135, 143
United States 19, 53, 59, 61,
    63–8, 74–5, 79, 83, 89,
    90, 93, 95–101, 106, 110,
    114
    California *10*, 59–61,
    67–71
    Oregon *11*, 24, 44, 53, 57,
    59, 61, 64, 93, 131, 142,
    149
    see also breeding, Native
    Americans, New England

Vaccinium spp. 10, 16–18, 49,
    134
    see also individual species/
    varieties
vodka 73, 110–11

wild berries *see* picking
wintergreen (*Gaultheria
    procumbens*) 17–18

witchcraft 33–6, *34*, *35*, 38, 40,
    121
        Wicca 40
wolfberry *see* goji
wonderberry *see* nightshade,
    black

zefir 104
zereshk *see* barberry